Aquarium Care Made Simple: Selected Success Tips

Contents

Introduction

Aquarium care can be simple, if you select the right tips and tricks that work for you and your fish. This book will provide you with some selected success tips for keeping your aquarium clean and your fish healthy.

Can You Manage An Aquarium With Salt Water?

An aquarium filled with salt water can be a lot of fun. Having it nearby has several advantages, one of which being the variety of fish you may stock it with and claim as your own. However, you may also discover that having this kind of tank has its drawbacks.

It's imperative that you spend some time contrasting these choices before deciding whether to go with a saltwater aquarium or a freshwater aquarium. Take the time to compare these possibilities.

Most people find it simpler to maintain and keep clean a freshwater aquarium. A saltwater aquarium will be more difficult to keep clean, but you will be able to put in a wider variety of fish and other animals.

Both a freshwater tank and the fish you stock it with will be less expensive. However, the salt water version offers a wider range of options. And because you may add a variety of different sea life critters that are not fish, you can even construct your own live ocean in your salt water aquarium.

For a salt water tank, you will have to put in more time and money. Additionally, you will have to invest more work in maintaining it. However, you should be aware that this kind of tank offers you a lot of rewards. You can use it to build an entirely new universe.

Even kids can learn about life in the ocean thanks to the tank in your house. Give your decision some thought. Examine the fish species you would most like to have in your salt water aquarium and assess your ability to give them the habitat they require to live in.

Fish Selection for Saltwater Aquariums

The choice of the fish you want to supply your saltwater aquarium with is your next duty after making that decision. Right now, you shouldn't go out and buy an aquarium. You must first carefully analyse the various options you have.

Although there are countless species, not all of them are suitable for an aquarium-like environment. Many of them would be better off in the water. However, there is one major reason why you should wait to purchase your aquarium before deciding what fish you will put in it. Of course, that is the size.

The size of the salt water aquarium you choose will depend on how many fish you have and how much space they require. It's crucial to take your time when picking out these fish. Take your time and make the best decisions if you are a novice aquarium owner.

Clownfish, damselfish, and mollies are some examples of fish that are simple to care for. Then you can include items like tangs, grammas, and triggerfish.

Before making a purchase, it's important to think about the more unusual options, such angelfish, anemones, seahorses, and even clams. These require a lot more maintenance and are frequently challenging for beginners.

Other aspects of the fish that you intend to keep in your salt water aquarium should be taken into account as well. You should take note of how well the different species will get along with one another.

Additionally, you ought to be aware of which are more hostile. When it comes to the water's temperature, salinity, and pH levels in the tank, in particular, you should be sure that they can all endure the same living circumstances. When selecting the fish species to stock your saltwater fish tank, keep these factors in mind.

How to Buy a Saltwater Aquarium

There are a number of factors you should take into account before buying your saltwater aquarium. First and foremost, you should give careful thought to the kinds of fish you want to keep as pets. Keep in mind that it is important to ensure that these creatures may coexist peacefully and that their respective needs for water are met.

When you are certain of the species you want to stock your tank with, you can look at the numerous alternatives for tanks you may buy.

The size of the tank should be your first priority. The fish will have more space to swim and live in a larger tank. This will enable them to perform as effectively as possible.

However, the more work it will require to keep the fish tank clean and at the proper levels for the fish, the bigger the tank will be. Most buyers of salt water aquariums go for models between 30 and 55 gallons in capacity. Do not forget to discuss the space requirements for your fish with the pet store employee.

Additionally, you want to seriously think about getting acrylic for your tank. Both stronger and easier to maintain, it is. Additionally, it will allow you to see more clearly. Next, think about where you want to keep your aquarium. The table or place will need to be stronger the larger it is.

Keep in mind to account for the water-filled tank's weight. Having a reef tank rather than a fish tank is another option to think about. These can give your fish tank additional detail and beauty if you have adequate space and the price is reasonable.

Even a kit that includes everything you need to set up and operate your fish tank is available for purchase. However, make sure that each of these is appropriate for your requirements.

Adding Water to a Saltwater Aquarium

You have carefully chosen the best saltwater aquarium for your needs, and you have carefully selected the fish to put in it. You need to take a lot of steps in order to fill your tank with the fish you actually want to see there.

You shouldn't find it too difficult to accomplish this, but you should be aware that in order for your fish to survive and grow in your salt water aquarium, you must gently fill the tank with water.

Start with wholesome fish first. Please examine them. Look they in good health? Do they have no trouble swimming around the aquariums at the pet store? Is the tank's water clean? Your salespeople at the pet store ought to be trustworthy.

Go somewhere else if you don't believe they are knowledgeable about what they are talking about. These fish might quite pricey at times! Avoid buying unhealthy fish for your aquarium.

Next, keep in mind to only add one or two fish at a time. Before adding the fish to the tank, make sure the appropriate levels are fulfilled. Make sure that the pH, salinity, and water temperature are appropriate for the species you have selected. You should understand that fish also dislike the change.

Before adding several fish to the aquarium, you must give them time to get used to their new surroundings. The best thing for you to do is to add a few fish every few days.

Make sure to feed your fish appropriately once they are in the tank. To do this, you must be certain that you are familiar with the fish's preferred foods and feeding schedules. Keep your fish in water that is between 75 and 80 degrees, feed them every three days, and give them a variety of meals like chopped-up shrimp and romaine lettuce.

Keeping Your Saltwater Aquarium Clean

Your saltwater tank contains fish that you are enjoying. You've done everything in your power to provide your new, little companions a wonderful place to live.

You must now keep it up. Keep in mind that keeping the tank clean is crucial to keeping your fish alive. To maintain your fish happy and healthy, you will need to take a number of steps.

You must first keep in mind to check the water in the tank every two weeks. The appropriate levels of ammonia, nitrate, nitrite, pH, and salinity must be checked.

Based on what your fish need when you bought them, you ought to be aware of what these stages are. The chemicals required to modify these levels are also available at pet stores.

Observe the water's salinity. It will typically be too high. Fill the tank with new, dechlorinated water to restore equilibrium. In the event that the salinity levels are too low, salt must be added to the water.

Each week, you should replace just 10 percent of the water in your tank with new, dechlorinated water. Take out and replenish 25% of the water in the tank every few weeks.

Finally, maintaining a clean aquarium for your fish is part of caring for your saltwater tank. It is important to keep the sides, top, and inside of the tank clean of algae while keeping an eye on the amount of algae present. As advised by the manufacturer, you should inspect the filter pads and the alkalinity.

You must remove the particles from both the water and the gravel. If you want to keep your saltwater aquarium a secure environment for your fish, you must take care of it.

However, you may achieve this pretty easily if you know what has to be done and develop a practise of doing it. As a result, it stops being a chore and starts to become enjoyable.

Choices for Aquarium and Fish Care

The freshwater fish in the Characidae family have a lot in common with them. They belong to the superorder Ostariophysi, which comprises about 68% of all freshwater species worldwide. The Weberian apparatus and a chemical that the fish releases when they are stressed both define this super order.

Central Africa has now been linked to the discovery of the family Characidae, which was first identified in South and Central America. The Characidae family has two primary subgroups: carnivorous and omnivorous.

The carnivorous species only consume meat, while the omnivorous species consume both plant and animal stuff. Although there are herbivorous Characidae as well, you should generally stay away from keeping them because they will devour every plant in your aquarium.

There are a few things you should consider before opting to maintain carnivorous Characidae. Be warned that anything smaller than the Characidae will be regarded as food first and foremost. Additionally, combining additional aggressive carnivores will only result in one of them being consumed.

With Characidae, you should raise significantly larger herbivorous fish. They will typically avoid anything larger than themselves, and unless provoked, the herbivore won't be interested in attacking. A Characidae will attack both alone and in schools, unlike the piranha, which has comparable jaws and feeding preferences.

Only schools tend to experience piranha attacks. However, both types might have a comparable impact on your hand, so use caution. For beginners, these fish are absolutely not the best choice.

Characidae that are carnivorous will consume almost any form of meat. Worms, smaller fish, etc. (many risky fish caretakers will fill the aquarium with a number of small, inexpensive fish so the predator has something to hunt).

Do not put your hands in the tank while feeding them, and try to avoid giving them a taste for red meat.

Rivers in South and Central America contain characidae, which reside there. The presence of a lot of peat and plant materials results in murky waters with an acidic PH. When cared for appropriately, Characidae will reproduce in captivity and lay eggs that adhere to the tank floor.

However, they will devour their young, so if you plan to try breeding Characidae, be ready to relocate either the adults or the young into a different aquarium as soon as they hatch.

White or spotted piranhas, also known as Serrasalmus Rhombeus, are another choice of those who enjoy keeping dangerous fish. Piranhas originate in South America's Amazon Basin, like Characidae.

Although they can reach lengths of up to 10 inches in the wild, most piranhas raised in aquariums only reach lengths of about 6 inches. Similar to Characidae, piranhas are not recommended for novices.

They cannot be kept with other fish because they are among the most aggressive fish. Their overly large jaw, which has a row of razor-sharp teeth, is their most noticeable characteristic. With powerful teeth, piranhas have been known to destroy aquariums.

You must take great care to keep your hands away from the fish at all times when netting a piranha. If you allow them, they will attack and rip apart your hand without hesitation. Your hand is just a little nibble for them because in the wild, a school of piranhas can quickly reduce a whole cow to bones.

Of course, piranhas consume meat. Any other fish maintained with them will be attacked and eaten. The fact that piranhas won't breed in tanks and their general disregard for water quality are some of the nicer aspects of keeping them. This stops piranha schools from showing up in your tanks.

In captivity, they will consume one another, especially if there are no other fish around to defend them. Only knowledgeable keepers should care for piranhas because they are quite aggressive and dangerous.

Support for Fish Care in Aquariums

The details of maintaining a healthy aquarium can be a little overwhelming for a newbie. The amount of jargon and machinery is enough to make anyone's head spin. It is advised to learn it all in pieces.

Many aspects of keeping aquariums need patience. Beginners are frequently advised to start with goldfish. The goldfish is one of the simpler fish to keep healthy and happy because it is widely available and highly attractive when in good condition. But be prepared to read a little. There arc words and processes to become used to.

No matter the type of fish, having an aquarium is essential necessary for maintaining healthy fish. Your aquarium needs to be properly cared for and maintained, and there are steps that must be taken each day and every week. Selecting the aquarium is the first step in caring for a goldfish.

Even though it's common to see goldfish kept in bowls and other small containers on television and even in real life, this is a horrible idea.

Even while a goldfish can survive for a while in a bowl that small, they won't actually thrive and will be more prone to illness and demise. The bare minimum aquarium size you ought to think about for a goldfish tank with filtration is ten gallons.

The fish are given plenty of oxygen by the filter flowing into the aquarium, which also agitates the water's surface and increases water oxygenation. The goldfish has more space to swim in and even some filtration currents to keep them happy and healthy.

Don't forget to factor in the amount of goldfish! More area will be needed if there are more goldfish.

Ask the staff at your neighbourhood pet store or aquarium shop for their recommendations (recommended). However, don't buy too many tanks at initially. Try to make things brief and uncomplicated. Inform them of the number of fish you plan to maintain and whether you want to add more later.

Before purchasing a product you are unfamiliar with, always conduct some research. There are many different products and accessories related to aquariums and fish. By doing some preliminary research, you can avoid purchasing unnecessary items.

Unless you have access to well water, chlorine or ammonia is likely present in your tap water. If you have particularly chlorinated water, these compounds are extremely toxic to your goldfish and may even result in their death. After filling the aquarium, you can purchase products that you can simply add thoroughly into your tap water.

They typically add substances to the water to help your fish produce its slime coat and fight off ick (a tiny parasite that is very frequent on stressed-out fish), as well as removing chlorine from the water.

There are various additives that bring necessary minerals back into overly pure water if you'd prefer to utilise distilled or reverse osmosis purified water.

Make sure to inspect the filters once per week and to wash them with some sort of dechlorinated water. For this, distilled water is OK. Snails frequently reside on filter media. Avoid crushing them, and take them out when you do your weekly cleaning.

These snails have a propensity to overbreed and consume all of the plant life in your aquarium, so it is not advised that you put them back in.

Additionally, it's important to maintain a relatively steady temperature in the aquarium. The water temperature can be moderately controlled with an aquarium heater. A thermometer for aquariums is also advisable to check the water's temperature.

Fish for freshwater aquariums

Aquariums might be attractive, but they can be expensive and difficult to maintain. It is strongly advised for beginners to stick with freshwater aquariums and fish.

Both freshwater and saltwater aquariums need some setup and upkeep, but freshwater aquariums are far less expensive and simpler to maintain. With freshwater, all you really need to get started is a tank, some pebbles or gravel, a light, a filter, a heater, and a thermometer.

For freshwater fish, simply fill it with water and let it sit for a few weeks to start a biological filtration cycle. Freshwater fish can be just as vivid and vibrant as their saltwater cousins if you chose them wisely.

Which Fish Shall I Purchase?

Which type of freshwater aquarium fish should I get? is perhaps the most frequent query a freshwater aquarium keeper receives. Fish in freshwater come in a variety of colours, sizes, and forms. Some can be maintained together while others cannot.

The easiest method to choose is probably to browse the selection at your neighbourhood aquarium store and see what appeals to you. The shopkeeper probably can assist you in ordering the items you desire if you don't see anything you like.

Additionally, make sure to research the compatibility of the various fish species you are thinking about keeping together.

Cichlids of various varieties and rainbow fish are popular choices for newcomers to keeping freshwater aquariums. Cichlids come in a variety of hues and can reach heights of about three feet in the wild.

Australian rainbow fish are typically colourful and highly attractive. A school of 4-5 Neons might serve the purpose of a tiny fish to complete your tank. They have virtually neon stripes on their otherwise clear bodies and never grow larger than large minnow size.

Maintenance and Care

You must monitor the PH of your water, which is a gauge of how acidic or alkaline it is, if you keep any of these fish. Different fish have varying levels of comfort, and some, like the Discus, can potentially perish if the PH is not perfectly maintained.

Make sure your body temperature is appropriate by keeping an eye on it. Tropical freshwater is where most of the most vibrant freshwater fish are found, and they need warm water to stay healthy and happy.

Support for Fish Care and Aquariums

1. **Know Your Fish**: Depending on whether your fish are freshwater or saltwater, their care may vary. The first category is also known as marine fish. The type of aquarium you give your fish depends on the category they belong to because saltwater fish require daily inspection to ensure their health in an unfamiliar environment.

Because of this, experts advise fish owners to watch each fish's behaviour patterns so that anything unusual can be noted and treated by a pet specialist.

2. **To establish a daily routine for your fish**, learn about their eating habits. Some fish may need frequent meals, while others can survive on just one meal each day. It's crucial to comprehend and interpret the dietary requirements of your fish.

3. **Try to maintain the aquarium water clean**; failing to do so could result in chlorine buildup and unclean circumstances for the fish. In addition to adding iodine salt twice weekly for marine fish housed in tanks, you can learn how to add calcium to aquarium water by investing in some reasonably priced water filters.

Additionally, removing algae accumulation in the aquarium that includes photosynthetic materials is crucial for the continued health of your fish.

4. **Filtering out at least 15% of the tank's water** on a weekly basis and replacing it with fresh, oxygenated water will help keep the water in the tank in the best possible condition and prevent the buildup of pollutants that could harm the fish.

Consult your neighbourhood pet store for guidance on the best filtration system to employ for your fishy friends' benefit as well as strategies to get rid of chemical buildup in your tank's water.

5. **Always try to clean and replace the water** after working to eliminate material from the tank, such as gravel. By purchasing a tester kit and buffer system that are readily available on the market, check the aquarium water for impurities like ammonia content, etc. every two weeks.

You can also use this to detect dangerous levels of other chemicals, such as copper, chlorine, and nitrate build-up, etc., as well as to determine the pH level.

However, keep in mind that fish naturally make nitrites, which are not hazardous to them. Instead, remove just the nitrous acidy salts that are toxic to fish. Add the helpful alkalinity build up test to these weekly tests once a month as well to assess the concentration in relation to the pH of the tank water.

6. Investing in a high-quality chemical, mechanical, or biological filter that your local pet store can advise you on is a wise way to prevent fish from becoming ill when kept in an aquarium environment.

It's also important to check to make sure these are functioning properly because a biweekly filter check can tell you when a replacement is due.

For more information, visit an online resource. For your fishy companions to breathe easily, keep your aquarium clean and your fish records up to date.

Aquariums and Gasteropelecidae Fish Care

For true fish lovers, purchasing an aquarium is more than just a hobby or passing fad. Deciding which aquarium to purchase largely depends on whether you plan to keep marine (sea fish) or non-marine (freshwater fish) species in the tank.

The fortunate thing about modern living is that we now have tanks equipped with switches that allow one to alter the temperature of the water contained therein, making for comfortable surroundings inside whether the tank light is intense or dim.

Modern tanks can benefit from the wide range of purification systems that are available for filtering out toxins and debris from the tank environment, helping to keep the water oxygenated and clean for the inmates in addition to temperature control.

The innovation in fish care for aquarium owners comes in the form of an automatic food distribution and fertilised dosage system, which eliminates the hassle of having to remember to feed the fish at the right times. Some of these innovations are mechanical, while others are electronic in nature.

Since there are so many different aquarium sizes, materials, and technologically advanced aquariums available on the market for keeping Piscean friends and botanical buddies in them, fish owners today are spoiled for choice when it comes to purchasing aquariums.

Of course, researching the 22,000+ species and their preferences when it comes to keeping fish healthy in a tank is sure to be a task, but an enjoyable one for those that love the hobby.

In addition to learning which species are dangerous and shouldn't be kept in captivity, such as Piranhas, learning about coldwater or tropical fish is vital for tank hygiene and fish health.

1. Flying fish, or Gasteropelecidae, such as the Hatchet fish, are primarily found in northern South America and are distinguished by their distinctly deep figures.

For this reason, tank owners are advised to keep a hood on the aquarium with flying fish in it to prevent them from escaping like they are prone to doing – at least 15 feet away from the tank! They are known as flying fish because of their affinity to raising the chest fins and attempting a float in the sky.

2. The Carnegiella Marthae, also known as the Blackwing Hatchetfish, is another species that shares characteristics with the first one and is native to the Amazon basin as well as Peru and Venezuela.

They typically only reach an inch or a quarter in length, have a black chest, ridge, and keel, and thrive in calm waters with other fish of the same species. The benefits of keeping this species of fish, which prefer soft waters and reproduce similarly to Hyphessobrycon, include a calm demeanour and simple eating habits.

3. The lower Amazonian regions are the home of the Silver Hatchetfish, Gasteropelecus Levis, which may grow to be an inch longer than the Blackwing species. Provided they are kept in a clean environment, they are typically unconcerned about sharing a tank with other fish.

Its breeding habits are currently being researched, much like the Blackwing variety, and little is known about them reproducing in tanks.

In addition to this family, the Cyprinidae, which includes carps and other related fish, is noteworthy. These fish typically have large bodies and bones and can be found throughout North America, Europe, some regions of Africa, and Asia.

Few of them have barbel fins, which make up for adipose fins; 8 feet is a typical size for them. Their pharyngeal bones also serve as teeth.

The Mahaseer, also known as the Indian carp, is one of the biggest freshwater carp breeds and occasionally exhibits characteristics similar to those of carps, such as round scales, soft fins, and toothless jaws in the minnow variety used as bait.

Aquarium at home

1. Potential owners of a home aquarium should conduct research on the species of fish that are simple to maintain and feed in addition to the many aquarium types they may purchase to make fish-keeping a pleasurable hobby.

Fish are quickly replacing puppies and kittens as the most popular pets because they are simple to care for. Pet stores are reporting higher demand than ever before for these finned friends, and this boom has caused local pet stores to expand into larger facilities and create a fish industry that didn't exist before.

Visit them when you have the opportunity; they are usually fantastic resources for learning more about options for fish keeping.

2. The neighbourhood pet shop is a good place to get useful information about various fish species, the care needed for their proper maintenance, and how to maintain tank conditions conducive to sharing space with other kinds of aquatic creatures.

There is a lot you can learn from the professionals at your neighbourhood pet store, from advice on the sources of bacteria and chemical build-up that can be harmful for the fish in a tank to learning about ways and means to prevent, control, and treat toxins and other substances that threaten the wellbeing of the aquarium fish.

Additionally, you can shop around and decide carefully what things you need to assemble a superb home aquarium and a system of support for your fish-keeping hobby. Both visiting the pet store owner in person and using the Internet are inexpensive and can provide better guidance at a lesser cost.

3. Maintaining a home aquarium requires the use of support devices like stands, temperature regulators, filters, lighting, and feeding assistants in addition to a host of others to ease your mind and keep the fish healthy. Fish-keeping as a hobby requires much more than simply buying the fish and putting them in an aquarium.

4. Research home aquarium care online or speak with a local pet store expert to reduce the intensive maintenance that keeping fish necessitates. Of course, you'll also need to know which species are unsafe to keep away from a child-friendly environment or at home.

How to Mount an Aquarium on the Wall

1. Many people who enjoy the sea and crave for the tranquil, relaxed, and quiet environment that having an aquarium offers them have long been fascinated by marine life.

However, keeping marine or freshwater fish is a different activity that has its own set of guidelines when it comes to keeping these species in a home tank environment. Hobbyists should educate themselves on these guidelines.

For instance, marine tanks can house tropical, cold-water, and exotic species as well as sharks and stingrays, but choosing a home for them also requires knowledge of their dietary demands and preferences.

2. Understanding the type of fish, such as freshwater or saltwater, will help you determine the type of tank needed to keep them, where to put it (based on cleaning requirements, such as accessibility for the same on a weekly or monthly basis), and what kinds of plants can be used inside the aquarium.

3. In addition to being a creative method to display your Piscean Pals, getting a wall-mounted aquarium is a definitive fashion statement.

These come in a variety of sizes and shapes, ranging from those the size of a TV screen to enormous walls enclosing the National Aquarium, Baltimore in Maryland.

Wall mounted tanks are trendy home decorations, but they do demand a certain level of skill and time in addition to patience to execute the job effectively.

4. The first step in selecting whether to install a wall-mounted home aquarium is to ascertain whether the walls of your house are sturdy enough to support the weight of such a novel fishkeeping idea: the strength of the walls will help you choose the size of wall studs to be used.

If at all possible, try to take this into account while building your home's foundation because only sturdy walls can support the concept of a wall-mounted fish tank.

5. You might think about hiring a professional services company to install your wall-mounted aquarium so that the hassle of having cables, pumps, and other equipment underfoot is avoided and a quality job is done.

This is a much more expensive option compared to doing it yourself for wall mounting an aquarium, but it's better than spending time, money, and effort you don't have right now.

Additionally, it gives you a way to pass any mistakes onto the company doing the job should accidents occur or home repairs be required.

In comparison to traditional fish tanks, which are prone to the hassles of cords and plugs getting underfoot and require more maintenance, wall mounted aquariums have a number of distinct advantages.

Homeowners can save valuable floor space, have added safety from children upsetting the tank, and enjoy the joy of having gay, colourful fish floating alongside them in a dream environment.

Diamond Aquariums

With the introduction of contemporary, inventive, and exquisite options in addition to a variety of aquarium owner accessories, the days of walking into a local pet store and just getting an ordinary tank with a hood and moving up to buying lighting and inhabitants for them are finally over!

Being an expensive hobby, investing in a jewel aquarium is not for the weak-hearted (or, for that matter, those without vast money).

Some people compare wanting to buy a jewel aquarium to going on a shopping trip to buy wholesale goods in a larger size or pack to save money instead of separately locating and fitting pieces or items.

This is because when buying a jewel aquarium (it gets its name from the manufacturer - a one-of-a-kind product at the moment), the dealer provides the buyer with all the possible support devices in one lot, which is a great deal!

Customers can choose from a wide range of different aquarium types and sizes when purchasing from one manufacturer, Jewel, but the dealer also serves as a supplier of accessories, offering a variety of aquariums with or without stands, equipped with filters, purifiers, and lights, among other things.

Aside from the magnificent Rio range of 125 litres to 400 litres, decorated and gravel-filled aquariums are occasionally in high demand. These aquariums can be installed into cabinets with heaters or other various equipment and range in size from 60 to 120 litres.

These jewel aquariums, which come in the colours of black and beech, are more affordable to purchase online than at the neighbourhood pet store. The Jewel Trigon series, which is the most expensive of the bunch and comes in model sizes of 190 and 350, is suited for mounting on stands or corner fitting.

The other series, known as the Jewel Vision variety, is available in sizes 180, 260, and 450 and has a curved glass front.

Even though they are heavy, all Jewel fish tanks have heating and filtration systems, making them an excellent investment for the price they cost. All Jewel aquarium cabinets are flat-packed for convenience, however they must be put together at home.

Aquarium care for freshwater and marine fish

1. Your strategy for acquiring and maintaining freshwater fish in your home aquarium should be founded on prior research and knowledge to direct your purchase of tank setup plan, which can be maintained entirely natural or have an ornate touch, depending on your preferences.

Naturally, from a scientific perspective, keeping fish captive means they are not really kept in a natural environment, but closely substituting these in the tank more than makes up for the lack of plants and their habitat in the wild.

2. Home aquarium owners will discover that these tank fish have a fantastic level of resilience and are able to easily adapt to different environments because it determines their capacity for survival.

3. Recognize that a sterile tank container is an instrument for separating fish from their advantageous biosphere, and learn how you, as a home aquarium owner, can work to incorporate these various organic parameters to mimic the fish's natural environments.

So that captive fish of any kind can survive here with the least amount of suffering.

It's crucial to gain knowledge of the techniques you can use to keep the living conditions in the tank for your fishy friends healthy, including understanding of water filtration, oxygenation, avoiding dangerous chemical buildup, and learning to spot changes in the eating habits of the tank inhabitants.

Therefore, a fish caretaker needs to be both a passionate hobbyist who enjoys caring for fish and an attentive individual who is focused on preventing unwanted situations in the aquarium.

4. Choosing between a framed fish tank and a basic one is totally up to the owner, but in a framed tank, which is often the preferred and less expensive alternative, care must be taken to ensure that the water is kept clean.

Some framed aquariums are made of plastic, while others are made of metal; in either case, the front is mostly composed of sturdy, water-resistant Plexiglas, which reduces the corrosive effect of chemicals and water, but accumulates scratches readily and gradually loses much of its clarity.

The other type of tank is composed of glass and lined with a silicone-based material that serves as an adhesive and can withstand any amount of wear and tear while remaining very flexible over time.

5. Home aquarium owners would do well to keep in mind that tank water accumulates acids and salts, which need to be regularly measured to test for dangerous levels to prevent fish from becoming ill.

Test kits and buffer units help to control and check for calcium and sodium build-ups that can be caused by toxic chemicals in addition to other apparatuses that are easily accessible in the market for judging quality of water, i.e. hard or soft, as well as other devices that are readily available.

These are significant investments for home aquarium owners because they need to know the water quality for the species of fish they have (freshwater fish may prefer spring, tap, or purified well water, whereas marine fish may prefer brackish or hard water).

So the owner needs to be aware of these and when to use chlorine-free water.

It will be much easier for owners to take care of their fishy friends if they use hydrometers to test the salt levels in the tank water, add 2-4 fractions of sea salt to every thousandth part of the tank water to increase brackishness for marine fish, know how to make water soft (add distilled water).

And know which species of fish require acidic water (yellowy brown in colour, can be made with chemical additives for reproduction stage of some fish).

Mollies, fish care, and guppy aquarium

The Mollies, which are easy to maintain in a tank environment and are members of the Poecilia family, are comparable to swordtail fish, which are members of the Xiphophorus helleri subgroup.

It has a larger fin than the swordtail, is referred to as, and mollies can be many different shapes and sizes, sometimes reaching up to 4 34 inches, with only the males being about an inch smaller.

The males and females differ in size, colouring, and gonopodium, but both sexes adapt to various living environments rather well.

Mollies can adapt to heat conditions between 72 and 82 degrees Fahrenheit, preferably in hard water conditions (pH level of 7 or 8), which calls for bright lighting, a certain amount of brackishness in the water, in addition to a variety of suitable plants.

Mollies live in an estuary habitat and can withstand a range of temperatures in a natural environment.

Mollies have a diet that includes algae and vegetables like spinach, and they prefer to be in places where there is a steady flow of water.

Due to their active personalities and capacity to adapt quickly to community tank environments, Mollies, which are livebearers, frequently reproduce in large numbers.

The Poecilia reticulata family of guppy fish, which are descendants of the Poeciliidae family and are primarily found in the waters of Guyana, Venezuela, and Brazil, are also found in the waters near Trinidad and Barbados.

Because of the favourable environmental conditions found there, which include temperatures between 68 and 75 degrees Fahrenheit and pH levels preferred by mollies.

The guppies can manage to survive in hard water as long as there is sufficient lighting, additional plant life, and a variety of meals made accessible to them in the tank setting.

Due to their loose-school personalities, guppies require continual movement. Despite the fact that they devour their young, guppies are nevertheless able to reproduce very easily in communal settings.

The first step in ensuring you are an informed hobbyist is learning about the fish that are easiest to keep in a home aquarium.

The next is learning about the various aquarium types that are available and which type is best to replicate a natural ecosystem while using cutting-edge technology to provide wholesome air and water conditions for the inhabitants of the tank.

The enormous aquarium market today has been transformed by innovative design technology, and aquariums now feature the best electrical circuitry, connectors, filtration and oxygenation systems.

As well as temperature control devices to adjust the water's temperature.

With today's enviable tank lighting options, owners can buy mechanical or automatic switches, automated feeders to make sure fish are fed on time, as well as a selection of additional accessories that make community living a comfortable choice for fish owners seeking variety in aquatic life.

Of course, it is advantageous to get knowledge of fish species, such as marine or non-marine species, tropical and coldwater fish, that can coexist peacefully with other sorts.

Setting Up Your Personalized Saltwater Aquarium

1. For those who enjoy keeping fish, getting a personalised saltwater aquarium and its inhabitants is a dream come true. However, understanding you can pick up a few tips from the pros can help you save money.

You may easily purchase the tank from your neighbourhood pet store to house your saltwater fish, and you can plan a rough budget for your project that includes ornamentation and accessories.

2. After purchasing the aquarium, the first thing to do is to clean it out.

It's equally vital to wash the various components with freshwater (without soap) and a soft cloth to remove any dust or chemicals that may have accumulated during storage and could hurt the fish.

3. Place the tank on a stable platform that is a little bit away from a wall so that the electrical cords and the plug outlet can be accessed without running the danger of an accident. This is important since regular fish feeding and cleaning will be necessary.

To prevent condensation from the saltwater tank from harming the stand, use a soft cleaning cloth close by the aquarium. Fill the tank with store-bought saltwater or create your own solution after making sure the installation is level.

Run all tank equipment for a few days to ensure proper operation and to determine the water's salinity, pH, and temperature levels for the types of marine fish you wish to maintain in the tank.

4. After testing the tank's water conditions, you can move on to the last stage, aquarium landscaping, by draining about half of the water and adding decorations like plants, fronds, and pebbles, etc.

Lowering the water level makes landscaping easier. Once this is resolved, you can once more replace the water that you had previously designated as the fill-line measure. (For this, use a permanent marker.)

It is strongly advised that before starting to keep an aquarium, a minimum of one month be set aside to determine the water's ammonia level and whether the conditions are suitable for the species of marine fish you want to keep there.

You can decide to do this with the saltwater fish already present in the aquarium or without them.

Use of an ammonia reducer will need you to repeat the procedure of determining the ammonia content in your tank's living circumstances, taking up valuable time that you could be spending relaxing and watching your marine companions swim around.

Fish Purchases for Freshwater Aquariums

1. As a home aquarium owner looking to buy freshwater fish, there are a few things to keep in mind. The most crucial is knowing which type of fish you want to keep and whether they can coexist with other fish of the same sort.

The number of fish you can comfortably keep in an aquarium depends on its size; as a general guideline, each fish needs at least 3 inches of space in each gallon of tank water so that they can develop organically.

Fish kept in freshwater aquariums only get as big as the area available to them, thus the bigger the tank you provide them, the longer they'll live!

2. Be familiar with your fish species. This is especially important if you have a freshwater aquarium setup since you need to know which species, along with other sorts, can live in captivity and what care they need to develop and reproduce.

Spend some time learning about the freshwater fish you want to buy, the type of tank environment that will work best for them, the ideal temperature for them, and the food they will be consuming. Aside from compatibility, these aspects also have an impact on the wellbeing of the fish in your tank.

3. When choosing fish for a non-marine aquarium, think about any benefits you can give the fish you buy, such as choosing fish that consume algae so the buildup does not affect tank upkeep and necessitates less work on your part.

4. Last but not least, it's crucial to know which fish species to avoid buying when thinking about buying fish for your freshwater tank. After all, you don't want the fish in your home aquarium to live in an environment of discord, do you?

Therefore, find out as much as you can about the species that are territorial, such as catfish, which can quickly grow large and suck up space needed by other fish in the tank.

Avoid purchasing fish that are harmful to keep in a freshwater aquarium, such as piranhas, since these can quickly contract sickness and intimidate the other fish in the tank. If you want to keep your fish happy, healthy, and for a long time, you should avoid this investment.

Cleaning Your Fish Aquarium's Algae

1. After you have set up your fish aquarium and have enjoyed watching the fish swim about under soft or bright lighting, you may also need to deal with scuff and algae build-up.

Which are inevitable consequences of keeping water in an enclosed space where marine residents live and various bodily secretions take place in addition to plant life.

Please note that this build-up of algae may occur in many locations throughout the aquarium and that it is not your fault. Sometimes, it occurs as a result of the tank's natural conditions, including the intensity of the light and the nutrients that encourage its growth.

2. To identify the type of algae developing in your fish tank, you must understand the nature of algae and the different types that can occur. You must also discover what causes algae to grow, what can kill it, and how to use chemicals to remove it from the fish tank if it does.

Since algae growth in the aquarium is a normal process, having this knowledge will help you remain on top of any build-up that you can manage, if not completely avoid.

3. Once you are aware of the nutrients causing the algae build-up, you can work to reduce or eliminate their levels to ensure that the algae do not have a favourable environment to flourish in.

You should also clean your aquarium as soon as you notice any other slime accumulating to maintain a clean aquarium and prevent it from ruining the healthy living conditions of the inhabitants. Start by replacing the tank's water, then advance to cleaning using chemicals designed to remove algae buildup.

4. Reduce the brightness and heat in your fish tank to avoid frequent algae build-up, use low light levels in it as little as possible, and, to be on the safe side, keep the aquarium out of direct sunlight since this can also cause algae build-up.

Algae build-up is greatly influenced by the lighting in the tanks. Naturally, if you get a family of fish that consumes algae, you will have found the ideal technique to reduce any build-up and also a way to expand your fish collection in the aquarium - so give it some thought!

You only have algae to lose, and everything to gain, including a stunning, spotless aquarium that will give you hours of enjoyment.

Cleaning and Maintaining a Saltwater Aquarium

1. Since the same fish in the ordinary marine life take excellent care of themselves, breed, and have long lives there, why should there be any unique need for aftercare when they are maintained in a home aquarium? This is the common misconception among tank owners.

However, this is where people err by failing to realise how important it is to properly clean and maintain a marine tank in order to keep the fish healthy in the future and to maintain its general upkeep.

Start by buying a device to keep the tank water clean—which, by the way, should only be filtered water—such as a reverse osmosis system, which you can find at your neighbourhood pet store or online.

The other option is to use standard water, adjust the temperature to the tank's marine fish species' needs, add chemicals to remove chlorine, and be sure to clean the tank at least once each month!

2. Maintaining your saltwater fish tank requires routine upkeep and cleaning, ideally once every two weeks. However, it's also crucial to realise that too much cleaning might remove beneficial microorganisms.

3. Please keep in mind that if your saltwater aquarium is fairly young, you should wait at least a month before adding fish, plants, or even decorations.

This time is for resting and testing the tank's water before the prisoners arrive. If you do not want to lose your beloved Piscean friends due to an imbalance in the water levels they generally favour, buy some cheap test strips to check the pH and chlorine levels in the tank water.

Don't remove gravel to clean the tank until you are confident the saltwater aquarium has been set up correctly and the water conditions are suitable for keeping fish and other marine species or even botanically adorning it. Doing so could upset the delicate chemical balance in the aquarium.

4. Any cleaning products you buy should be carefully considered as beneficial and safe for the health and cleanliness levels of the tank's inhabitants. They should also be successful at cleaning the saltwater aquarium without disrupting its chemical balance, especially if you have an acrylic tank.

5. You can use phosphate drops to clean the water in your marine fish tank, which prevents build-up too fast, or you can buy a pair of hermit crabs and snails to keep algae at bay. Learn about the simplest ways to clean tanks and limit build-up of debris and algae that dirty up the saltwater aquarium.

These adaptable marine organisms are frequently called to as a tank's cleaning staff because they also remove rocks and gravel from the tank.

As algae is tough to remove with just any cleaning instrument, you can spend money on a decent set of gloves, a scraper, or a scratch pad to shine the glass for yourself.

Finally, if you are using a filter, keep in mind that the optimal direction to aim it is downward, into the tank water, to prevent the buildup of too much salt on the aquarium's lid.

Learn about the best water filter for your tank needs, the conditions that encourage the growth of algae, and the ideal tank lighting (no more than 6 hours per day at a set time, keep tank out of direct sunlight, etc.) for the type of marine fish you have so you'll know what to avoid and what procedures to follow for good marine tank hygiene.

Buying an Aquarium: Saltwater Aquariums from A-Z

1. Remember, there is no shortage of variety when it comes to the types of aquariums you can purchase for housing saltwater inhabitants.

There are only two main considerations you should take into account: your budget and the time and effort you can spare to learn about the potential inhabitants of your marine tank and whether you are up to seeing to their regular upkeep.

2. There are many different saltwater aquarium kinds, sizes, and decoration options available.

Which ultimately leads to consumers feeling that they have a lot of options and the idea that there is no surefire recipe for success. Fish tank aficionados may find it challenging to choose the right kind of fish tank while constructing a saltwater aquarium.

Before stepping foot inside a pet store, anyone who has any plans to put up a fish tank should think about a number of variables.

3. The size of the tank should be taken into account next. If you're a newbie, you should choose a modest aquarium and focus on keeping the tank and its occupants clean. Within a few months, you should have a decent sense of how many fish a specific size aquarium can hold and how to care for it.

4. Make sensible fish selections for your aquarium. Make sure the saltwater carnivorous fish in the tank have enough of room to swim around if you plan to have even a small variety of them. The little kind of shark will get hostile and harm the other exhibit fish in the tank if the tank is crowded and small.

5. Make a sensible choice for the tank's construction material. Glass and acrylic are the two materials used to make aquariums. Glass is a superior option because it is harder to scratch, but care must be taken to avoid cracking.

Because acrylic is so readily scratched while cleaning an aquarium, you will quickly feel the need to replace it, which is a costly proposition.

6. In a 2 cubic foot tank, you should never keep more than 10 fish. Purchase a larger tank if you wish to keep more fish.

7. Natural greenery ought to be used in the tank. Avoid using artificial aquarium plants since the natural ones assist clean the water and serve as a breeding ground for germs that fish consume.

8. Make sure the tank has a water filter and an aerator. There are several readily available electric accessories to choose from.

9. A vital component of an aquarium is gravel. It improves the aesthetics of the tank in addition to assisting the water filter in maintaining clean water.

10. It should be well-lit but not overly so. It will do to use a little fluorescent tube. Before putting fish in your tank, make sure it contains all of these extras. If any of these are absent, your aquarium will not be complete.

Should I Get A Saltwater Aquarium?

One of the most sought-after types of fish tanks is the salt water aquarium. It gives you the option to keep a greater range of fish, many of which are attractive and enjoyable options to create, despite the fact that it can be more difficult to really maintain and even more expensive.

However, you should be aware of the distinctions between these two types of aquariums if you are thinking of installing this type of fish tank in your house or place of business.

Deciding

Knowing which types of tanks will provide you the fish you want is the most important factor in choosing the sort of tank to have. For instance, you should only use freshwater tanks if you wish to own goldfish.

On thc other side, choose salt water if you'd like to acquire a clownfish. Take the time to look at a few species to see which ones might simply work the best for your needs and desires if you have no idea what kinds of fish you would like to acquire.

You should be aware that these tanks differ from one another. The freshwater aquarium will be simpler to maintain because there isn't any salt to worry about. Additionally, it will have more fish in its aquarium.

Of course, it also gives you access to the fish that are available at the lowest prices. Consider saltwater fish aquariums if you're searching for something a little more difficult and rewarding as well.

You have a greater selection of fish to choose from, despite the fact that they do need more labour on your part. Additionally, you will be able to design your own tiny ocean with a variety of marine life in it.

Take into account factors like your spending limit and the quantity of time you have to devote to caring for these fish. You might also want to think about how much space you have available for the fish tank.

While a smaller saltwater aquarium is possible, many people choose to have much larger aquariums. Although relatively normal, this calls for that much more care and demands.

Make sure to carefully consider your options in order to make the best decision for your requirements. If you decide to go with a salt water aquarium, there are many options available that are just waiting for you to discover them.

How to Maintain Your Saltwater Aquarium

You will need to take care of your salt water aquarium in a number of ways. It makes sense to spend some time learning about the things you need to do to maintain your tank since you recently paid a significant amount of money into both the aquarium itself and the fish you intend to populate it with.

While doing so is not inherently difficult, it is something you must do if you want to keep your tank operational and your fish investment profitable. But doing it is not difficult.

Here is a checklist of the tasks you must complete to keep your salt water aquarium functioning at its peak, for your convenience.

- Every two weeks, test the water. The water needs to be tested for a number of things. These consist of the concentrations of ammonia, salinity, pH, nitrite, and nitrate.

Testing for these things is simple and just takes a few seconds. Prior to buying your fish, you should simply find out what the usual quantities of these substances should be from the pet store employee.

- Baking soda can be added to water one spoonful at a time to lower pH levels if they are too high. Before adding additional, make sure to give it time to thoroughly dissolve.

- You may simply raise the salinity of your water if it is too low by adding salt to it.

- You will need to add dechlorinated water to the tank if your salt level is excessive, which is frequently the case. This occurs naturally as the tank's water starts to evaporate. The salt concentrations in the remaining water will be levelled.

- Iodine and calcium should be added to your tank at the proper concentrations. Speak with your fish clerk about the proper amounts so you'll know what to do and how often. These are typically unique to the species of fish you possess.

- 10% of the water in your fish tank needs to be removed once a week and replaced with brand-new, dechlorinated water. The water will stay clean as a result.

- Remove 25% of the water from your tank once or twice a month, and replace it with new, dechlorinated water.

- Unless you have fish that require a different temperature, keep your water between 75 and 80 degrees.

- The tank needs to be maintained as well. Keep algae off the tank's interior cover and walls, inspect the filter pads, and do any necessary alkalinity tests. Additionally, you must clear out the extra gravel in the tank.

By following these tips, you can keep your saltwater aquarium operating at its best and keep your fish content.

Why Select A Saltwater Aquarium

There are many advantages to having a salt water aquarium. You could be prepared to transition from freshwater fish tanks to ocean life if you are used to browsing the department store and picking out the ideal tiny goldfish to bring home with you.

Of course, there are a lot of distinctions between the two types of tanks. The variety of fish that can be kept in an aquarium is the main cause of this. However, there are many more justifications for choosing a saltwater aquarium over a freshwater aquarium.

Put the goldfish back down after taking a step back. You should now investigate marine life.

The Advantages To Think About

- You have access to a bigger selection of fish. Regardless of what anyone claims, you might be able to keep more interesting species in your saltwater aquarium than in any kind of freshwater aquarium.

They are frequently far more interesting to look at from a distance, more colourful, and have a wider variety of forms and sizes.

- Additionally, you'll be giving yourself a small task. You'll probably need to spend a little more time taking care of your fish tank in the salt water aquarium.

Depending on the type of fish you own, you will need to check the water's quality and salt content on a daily or weekly basis.

Additionally, you must assess the condition of your fish. This will get you more respect and adoration for your small guys in a matter of seconds.

- A saltwater tank has advantages for kids too. You will be able to instruct them about ocean life if you provide them a sizable one. You may build a world above sea level that is as amazing and packed with knowledge that kids will love to study, in addition to building an aquarium to house the fish you love.

The salt water aquarium is an option available to you. You will undoubtedly discover that keeping fish in a freshwater tank is less expensive. You won't, however, find them to be more fascinating and entertaining than the fish in this salt water aquarium.

Selecting A Saltwater Aquarium

Your task is to choose the salt water aquarium that best suits your requirements when making this decision. You can discover that there are numerous aquarium types to pick from, including various sizes and materials.

However, if you contrast your possibilities, it will become clear that you must carefully take your demands and preferences into account.

The salt water aquarium should be carefully chosen, and it's always a good idea to make sure your decision is one you can truly maintain.

The Content

The type of material from which the salt water aquarium will be created is the first thing you must decide. You have mostly two options. First, there is glass as an option. This is the less expensive option out of the two and has a respectable capability.

You may also clean it quickly. A different choice is acrylic. Now, these are typically superior options because they are much stronger than glass and allow for better visibility than glass.

However, the fact that acrylic aquariums can be acquired in a variety of forms and sizes so you may have them perfectly fit in your home is arguably the most significant reason to think about them.

For saltwater fish, you shouldn't use anything like a glass bowl or vase because they are too small and harmful.

Size Matters, Too

The size of the saltwater aquarium you choose should also be taken into account. Your fish will have a better time in the aquarium the bigger it is. Additionally, it might offer them a better living situation.

However, the cost and difficulty of maintaining it will increase with its size. For this work, you should typically stick with tanks that are between 20 and 55 gallons.

You should also give serious thought to the kinds of fish you intend to keep in the tank. Each fish will require a particular size of space to call their own. Different fish will require different amounts of space to swim. Select the appropriate aquarium for the types of fish you want to keep.

Last but not least, be sure to consider the weight of the tank while selecting the appropriate aquarium. You should probably make sure the table you use to set the tank on can support the weight of the tank when it is filled with water and fish. Make sure your tank is sturdy enough to support this as well if you choose to embed it in a wall.

How To Begin A Saltwater Aquarium

Once you've made the decision to possess a saltwater aquarium, you'll want to get right to work on buying and stocking your tank. But when it comes to these tanks, there are a few things to take into account.

You'll want to make sure that you give your fish (your expensive fish, mind you) the best possible room for their needs because this will function as their home.

Here are some simple guidelines to follow when selecting the best aquarium and making the most of your money.

- **Select the varieties of fish you want to keep**. Because each fish will need a different amount of space in your aquarium, you should tackle this first.

You'll need to invest in a bigger aquarium for yourself if you really want to keep a bigger fish. You should avoid wasting money on an aquarium that is far too large if you just intend to buy tiny species.

- **Depending on your demands, choose your tank**. You must ensure that your tank is strong enough to support the volume of water it will hold, that it is well constructed so that you won't have any issues, and that it is placed on a surface strong enough to support the weight of the tank when it is full of water.

You must also choose the right tank based on the types of fish you plan to keep in it.

- **Examine the cost**. When it comes to salt water aquariums, there are numerous options. You might be tempted to buy the one you saw at the neighbourhood pet store. However, you might want to look into your alternatives in other places as well before making this decision.

The correct kind of aquarium might be found at a garage sale or even a used shop if you know what you're searching for, but this is challenging to do. Instead, think about using the internet to locate the best aquarium price.

You can also think about getting a saltwater aquarium kit. However, these can be pricey. The kit might be more valuable if you require everything in it than it would be if you had to buy each component separately. But in most situations, it is a choice that you must make.

Your Saltwater Aquarium's Filling

After deciding on your saltwater aquarium, you may start working on stocking it with the species you want to own. However, you should think about your options carefully before moving forward.

Your aquarium can contain a lot more than just fish. But keep this in mind. Whatever you decide to put in the tank, be sure your fish will still have enough space to swim around whatever they choose.

If your tank is smaller than average, you might need to restrict what you put in it. But think about your possibilities.

Actually, you have more options for stocking your saltwater aquarium than just your fish. Instead of merely getting a fish tank, you might want to think about getting a reef tank.

However, if you are new to keeping fish, a conventional tank may be considerably simpler to manage and clean. The reef tank will undoubtedly be helpful if you're up for a bigger challenge.

You may get some really stunning features from this tank, such coral and anemones. If you want, you can even build your entire tank around these components.

Next Fish

The fish is the next thing you should think about. The finest species to begin with in a saltwater aquarium are damselfish, mollies, and clownfish.

Because of their size, survival potential, and simplicity of maintenance, these fish are the greatest beginner fish. When you've finished, you can add additional fish, such as grammas, triggerfish, tangs, and even wrasses.

Always take in mind the number of fish and the size of the aquarium. Hermit crabs, shrimp, and sea urchins are all options if you want to include something outside regular fish.

Novices Beware

You've seen them and wish you could own them, but creatures like eels, jellyfish, seahorses, angelfish, and anemones are incredibly difficult to keep alive.

Before spending money on one of these if you really want to possess one, make sure you improve your fishing skills via actual practise.

Always make sure your fish are entirely healthy and come from a healthy-looking tank when you go to buy them.

Don't buy from your local pet store if you enter and wonder what smells awful, what is floating in the water, or if you are unsure that the salesmen are knowledgeable about their products. The fish probably won't live for very long.

Saltwater Aquariums: Important Questions

You should spend some time doing numerous things when looking for the ideal fish for your saltwater aquarium. You should first be aware of what you are looking for. Spend some time getting to know the fish that will get along well in your tank.

You should also consider how much space they require and the kind of care they will require from you. You can learn a lot of things right now on the internet. But there are a few questions you should put to your salesperson before you buy the fish when it comes to actually stocking your saltwater aquarium.

Never forget to get your fish from a reputable pet store. With the quality of the fish they offer, you should feel secure.

If you have any reservations about the shop and intend to buy pricey fish from them, think very carefully before you act. You may most likely find a better place to buy your fish.

Having said that, there are a few questions you ought to have regarding the fish you intend to get for your salt water aquarium.

These are a few.

- **What kind of care should you give the fish?** In most situations, you'll need to understand the fundamentals of this. You must be aware of the fish's demands as well as what it has become accustomed to while residing in the pet shop. When you get the fish home and put him in your tank, this can help him survive better.

- **What kind of food, how much, and when should the fish eat are all important questions.** Once more, both the pet store and the animal may be unique in this regard. But the main thing is to make sure you feed your pet fish the highest-quality food you can.

- **What standards of water quality do fish require?** You should be aware of the specific pH level, salinity, and water temperature requirements for this plant. You must make sure that your tank can accommodate all of these requirements and that the levels required for this fish match those required for the other species you already have there.

Finally, inquire about the fish's aggression with your salesperson. You must determine whether a fish will get along with another fish or if they will attack one another. Actually, it really is that easy!

By knowing this information, you can optimise the performance of your saltwater aquarium. You'll be equipped with the knowledge required to run a prosperous aquarium as well.

Aquariums with saltwater: Adding Fish

You might be prepared to go and eager to swiftly fill your salt water aquarium when it comes to adding fish. You just made a large financial investment in your tank.

You might have even bought something beautiful that you now want to have fish in. However, you really do need to know a few things before you start so that you don't just head to the pet store and buy a bunch of fish to throw into your tank.

By doing this, you can ensure that your fish have the best possible chance of thriving in their saltwater aquarium.

Realizations...

You need to be aware of a few facts regarding the fish that will soon reside in your aquarium. To begin with, not all fish can coexist in the same tank.

Certain fish will require particular salinity, pH, and even water temperature conditions. You must locate fish that can withstand the similar conditions. Additionally, certain fish are aggressiver than others. You do not want the large, strong one to take out your pricey fish.

Another thing to keep in mind is that you should make sure your fish are adding steadily to the tank. Fish don't take change well. Both the water they will be in and the water they were just in need to contain the same kinds of components.

Only a few fish at a time should be added to the aquarium. When adding them, you should always check to see that the levels of ammonia and nitrite are zero. Typically, this will take place following a tank cycle.

Remember to consider how many fish you ought to keep in that aquarium as well. You should keep this in mind as a general rule. You can keep up to three inches of fish in your aquarium for every ten gallons of salt water.

If you want to keep your fish for a long time, you must provide them these things. By taking these actions, you are allowing the fish to become adjusted to their new environment and providing them the best chance to live.

There is no reason not to achieve the greatest outcomes from your aquarium if you will be investing money on fish.

Aquariums with Saltwater: Understanding Your Fish

You're finished once your saltwater aquarium is filled with fish, right? That is not the situation. There are still tasks for you to complete, such as learning more about your fish. All fish are unique from one another, just like people.

While some people prefer to eat at set times, others prefer to eat whenever they feel like it. Only one thing is certain. You will need to take care of every element of their care, just like you would with kids.

But this might be more than just a chore. It can even be extremely entertaining and fun. You must devote time to caring for your fish if you keep them in salt water tanks.

If you have a skilled and trustworthy pet store employee, you can learn the majority of what you need to know about your salt water aquariums from them. Before bringing your fish home, you'll want to be aware of a few things.

For instance, you should be aware of the fish species that can coexist in your aquarium. You should be aware of the kinds of water—including pH, salinity, and temperature requirements—that fish require to survive.

All of the fish you keep in your tank should have comparable requirements for these things.

You'll need to feed them once you've got them in there. Although this varies for each species, saltwater fish typically need to eat every three days. This is something you should be aware of before buying your fish.

You should also be aware of their food preferences.
Some people will demand that you give them a varied diet that includes foods like chopped shrimp and even romaine lettuce. They can maintain a balanced diet thanks to this.

You ought to be able to keep track of any variations you occasionally see in your fish. Thus, you must observe the animal while it swims and eats and become familiar with its typical behaviour. The fish can be ill if you notice something is off or something seems unusual.

This might be brought on by the water the fish is in, among other things. You can buy a variety of items to place in your tank to support their recovery or continued health.

Any issues you may have can be discussed with your veterinarian to find out what is precisely advised.

It's also vital to remember that fish just do not have the same longevity as humans have. Consequently, you should prepare to replace them as well.

Upkeep of Your Saltwater Aquarium

Your salt water aquarium cost you a lot of effort and money to build. Now that you are prepared, you can fill it with the fish you have always wanted to own.

However, simply because you are stocking it with the fish you desire does not mean that you are finished caring for it. The main reason fish in salt water aquariums pass away is that the water is of inadequate quality.

You must be careful to keep the water quality in the tank in order to properly care for your fish. Your biggest responsibility even is this.

To do this, however, there are a number of steps you must take in order to guarantee the finest water quality and ideal conditions for your fish. Every two weeks, you'll need to test a number of things in your tank.

If you recently filled your fish tank with water or introduced a new fish, you shouldn't conduct this experiment. The water quality will be immediately affected by these items.

Check:

- Levels of Nitrate

- Levels of Salinity

- pH values

- Amounts of Ammonia

- Nitrite content

You must be aware of what your fish require in order to determine whether these levels are appropriate. Before even buying your fish, you ought to be aware of this.

To ensure that all the different species of fish you put in the salt water aquarium agree on these levels, you need learn what needs the fish have. Now, if the levels are not where they ought to be, you should get the proper chemicals to assist in bringing them into balance.

These are available online or at your neighbourhood pet supply store that carries fish. If your pH levels need to be raised, add a spoonful of baking soda to the tank to make the necessary adjustments.

Add table salt to the water when you need to raise the salinity level. You can add dechlorinated water to the tank to balance out any overly salty water, which is frequent, if it exists.

Maintaining your saltwater aquarium will stop feeling difficult and start feeling more like an activity that is natural and usual. Taking care of your fish is an excellent way to get to know them better and engage with them. You may be enthralled by their attractiveness.

14 Simple Tips for Keeping a 55 Gallon Freshwater Aquarium in Good Condition

A 55 gallon fresh water aquarium is a wonderful choice when you decide to buy a new aquarium. Its size allows it to hold multiple fish at once while still fitting into small spaces in your home or place of business.

Here are some straightforward suggestions to help you learn the fundamentals of aquarium upkeep, while your neighbourhood stores may very well be able to help you with all the nuances involved with these kinds of aquariums:

1. One should always choose an acrylic tank over a glass aquarium when building a 55 gallon freshwater aquarium. The reason for this is that acrylic tanks are much lighter and simpler to handle. Additionally, the acrylic tanks are more visible than the glass tanks.

2. Prior to buying your fish tank, be important to buy a proper support so that you may position it safely and correctly.

3. To maintain the fish tank, you would require a number of tools, such as a heater and thermometer to monitor the water's temperature.

4. About five bags of rocks would be needed for a typical 55-gallon freshwater fish tank. You can choose from a variety of alternative substrates if you need to line the bottom of your tank. To make your fish tank more appealing, be sure to use a particularly vibrant colour.

5. To ensure that the water in your fish tank is clean and healthy for your fish, you would also need a filter to go on top of the tank. Because there are so many different types of filters on the market, experts generally suggest doing thorough research before buying a filter. Your fish tank's type will solely determine the sort of filter you buy.

6. There are some filters that are positioned at the side of your aquarium, while others are positioned beneath the substrates that make up the tank's bottom. It's not always necessary to purchase the most costly filter because they might be very pricey. The simple filters are frequently adequate as well.

7. The proper lighting would also be necessary for your aquarium. The fish react positively to light, however they require a balance of in and out lights. You have the choice of keeping the fish tank's lighting fairly simple or changing to more advanced settings. Turning on the basic light for a few hours each day is ideal for the majority of fish species.

8. Make sure there are enough plants in your fish tank. In addition to making the fish tank more attractive, they also help to purify the water by absorbing pollutants and adding oxygen. Water and ammonia are broken down by the water plants. The bacteria-containing fraction of the bad or contaminated water is then removed by these plants together with the ammonia.

As fish emit a lot of ammonia, plants keep the chemical equilibrium in the fish tank in check. The fish also enjoy hiding out among the vegetation. You can put many different kinds of fresh water plants in your 55 gallon aquarium.

9. You can also choose to buy plastic plants if you don't want to deal with the inconvenience of live ones. The variety of synthetic plants that are currently available is so astounding that your fish will never be able to distinguish between the actual and the plastic plants, until and until the fish try to eat the plants.

10. You can pick from a wide selection of beginner fishes once the aquarium is ready to receive your fish. If you want to begin with resilient fish, consider maintaining live bearers like barbs, gouramis, and danios. These fish have the innate ability to manage the high nitrate concentrations in your fish tank.

11. Wait a month, or 30 days, before adding new fish to the tank with these buddies to give the older fish time to adjust.

12. Keep an eye on your fish otherwise you might not notice any symptoms of illness or agitation. Such symptoms typically don't appear for 30 days.

13. If you don't take care when transferring your new fish and follow the advice of the pet store where you bought them and some trained hobbyists, you risk making the fish sick.

14. A 55 gallon fresh water aquarium should be able to accommodate a total of 15 to 20 tiny fish. Make sure your fish tank allows them enough room to play and grow in a healthy manner.

22 Things to Keep in Mind When Knowing Your Fish and Aquarium

You must first learn how to maintain your aquarium, including caring for your fish and keeping it clean, once you have gathered all the ingredients needed for one.

You must thoroughly research the market and compile all the available information before making the aquarium's material purchases.

Among the supplies needed to build an aquarium are:

Aquarium or container

Filters

Heaters

Gravel

Floss

Buffers

Food

and Fish

Here are some useful hints to assist you in better maintaining the fish and the aquarium:

Heaters

1. These are crucial for keeping tropical fish healthy.

2. However, you must verify their dimensions and that they precisely fit in your aquarium before buying the filters and heater.

3. They must not take up any extra room.

4. If your tank is too small to fit in these, a larger tank will be necessary.

Materials Necessary

An aquarium necessitates a number of additional purchases for accessories and routine upkeep. These include things like plants, gravel, food, decorations, test kits, water treatment, and more.

All of these materials serve a variety of functions, such as maintaining the natural resources in the fish tank with gravel, adding colour to the décor with ornaments, making the fish feel at home with plants, and ensuring the survival of your fish with food.

The test kit monitors the water's purity. Since most locations' tap water is not sufficiently pure to be utilised in aquariums, water treatment becomes essential.

Here is the aquarium construction process:

1. Fill a bucket with water first, then rinse the pebbles to remove any dirt, filth, or bacteria.

2. When the gravel has been cleaned, add water to your tank.

3. Add the remaining half of the water that the tank actually needs.

4. The aquarium's decorations and plants should then be added.

5. This completes the aquarium's need for additions.

6. Finally, fill the tank to the desired level with water.

7. Use the instruction manual that came with your tank now. Fill your tank correctly by adhering to the guidelines provided in this manual.

8. Place the heating and filter systems in the tank next.

9. Follow the directions in the handbook you were given when you received the heater and filters in order to install them safely and effectively.

10. The water treatment system is then added to the tank. By doing this, dangerous substances in the water, such as copper, metal, and other associated elements, are removed.

11. Now either utilise specific materials that allow you to do that safely before adding the fish to the tank, or else we advise you to wait at least a few weeks before adding life to your tank.

12. There are some naturally occurring microorganisms in a tank of water. To keep your fish healthy and secure, the water needs to be filtered to remove these microorganisms. Once the aquarium's water has settled, use your test kit to see if it is completely clean or not.

You should also check that the water is the proper temperature and that all of its chemicals are in balance.

13. Add your fish in small amounts after the water in the tank has been checked one last time.

Learn your fish

I suggest adding the following fish species to your aquarium:

1. Damsel is a saltwater fish and is the one that is most frequently suggested.

2. Keep in mind that the dominant fish will always eat the weaker fish. So, since the water is salt, we advise you to put some aggressive fish—exactly, only two of one kind—and then add others gradually.

3. It is advised to avoid choosing passive fish if you decide to keep some freshwater fish.

4. However, you cannot have freshwater fish and saltwater fish in the same tank, therefore you might think about keeping two distinct tanks.

5. I recommend fish for beginners like the white cloud mountain minnow, goldfish, danio, etc.

6. Additionally, you can consider getting a passive fish with a bristle nose. It expands by about 5.5 inches.

7. The otocinclus is a passive fish that resembles bristle noses and develops to a length of around 2 inches. Otocinclus adores living in regions with plants and rocks.

8. Another passive fish, Plecostomas, develops to a length of around 24 inches and dwells on and among rocks and vegetation.

9. Other passive fish species are Veitail and Marble. Both of these grow to a height of around 6 inches and adore living among and near plants and rocks.

25 Simple Tips for Maintaining Your Goldfish Aquarium

There are many pastimes that one might engage in that may one day become true passions. Keeping an aquarium is one of them.

However, this pastime is serious because there is no room for error or you risk hurting or killing a living thing.

A goldfish is a gorgeous and enjoyable fish to keep in your aquarium. Here are some simple guidelines to remember so you can keep a cute pet for many years in your lovely aquarium:

1. A goldfish has a lifespan of 5 to 10 years, depending on how well you take care of it.

2. A good rule of thumb is to wait to buy the fish until you have finished preparing the aquarium for your new companion.

3. Give the fish enough of food so that it can live a long and healthy life.

4. Ensure that the water in the tank is consistently clean and fresh.

5. Make sure your tank is completely prepared and has everything needed in it before introducing fish.

6. Make sure the gravel you add to the tank is completely clean before you start setting it up. Fill a pail with water and rinse the gravel to remove any dirt, filth, or bacteria before cleaning it.

7. Keep in mind that goldfish are fairly filthy animals, so keep the gravel layer very thin.

8. The aquarium's decorations and plants should then be added.

9. Check that all of the additives are in the tank and that they are clean and well washed before adding any water.

10. Since goldfish are a very active species, allow them enough room in the tank to swim.

11. Don't forget to make one or two hiding places for the fish as well. This would give it a lively feel.

12. Finally, fill the fish tank with water.

13. Make sure to place a dechlorinator in the tank because your fish may be poisoned by the chlorine in regular tap water.

14. Turn on the filter after the fish tank is ready. Additionally, make sure that the filter must be replaced frequently to maintain the health of your fish.

15. You would require a heater because goldfish prefer a room-temperature environment. A goldfish prefers a temperature range of 68 to 80 degrees. Additionally, goldfish cannot tolerate any sudden changes in temperature.

16. Before introducing the fish, you can choose to leave the filter running in the tank for a day or two so that it can remove any bacteria or germs that may have gotten into the water, gravel, or additives.

17. Now gradually introduce the fish to the tank. Actually, the ammonia that the fish produce first renders the water unfit for the fish to dwell in, and it takes time for the cleansing process to settle down. Your fish may perish if you fill the tank with too many fish at once.

18. Additionally, the water in the gold fish tank begins to create some really helpful bacteria as time goes on, making your fish very healthy, but it is a very laborious process. These bacteria largely transform the hazardous compounds that the fish that inhabit the area emit into useful ones. The key is to simply start with one fish, so to speak.

19. Also, you should be aware that adding fish to the tank is necessary for the nitrogen cycle to start. Therefore, operating the empty tank for a number of days would be useless.

20. You should think about replacing about 25% of the water in the new fish tank every few days. For at least the first two weeks or so, this must be done.

21. All pet stores sell goldfish food, so you can get it anywhere. Make sure to buy some food for your first goldfish when you buy it. Keep in mind that the first few times you should only feed modest amounts of the meal.

22. The food that is still there sinks to the bottom and eventually rots away. This food goes bad and produces compounds that are so toxic they can kill your fish. Therefore, make an effort to keep the fewest amount of food. The key to doing it successfully is to feed your fish while keeping an eye on them. Put in as little food as it eats in the first 2-3 minutes, and only do this twice per day. Always read the goldfish's food label that you receive when you buy a fish if it pertains to food.

23. The fish tank's nitrogen cycle converts harmful compounds that are produced there into beneficial ones by removing the toxic ones. This cycle produces foam, which temporarily clouds the water. You shouldn't be concerned if this happens because it is a natural process and instead shows that the tank is safe for the fish.

24. Additionally, make sure the water in the tank is completely clear before adding any additional fish.

25. Goldfish can get rather big as they get older, thus their swimming space in the tank needs to be increased. If the tank is overcrowded, your fish may become ill and perhaps perish.

If you follow these recommendations, we are confident that your fish tank will make a suitable aquarium for your goldfish.

20 simple suggestions for aquarium maintenance

There are many pastimes that one might engage in that may one day become true passions. Keeping an aquarium is one of them. However, this pastime is serious because there is no room for error or you risk hurting or killing a living thing.

The first and most important thing you must realise before deciding to take care of an aquarium and its fish is that you must first prepare the aquarium and make it suitable for the fish to live in before you buy the fish.

You must be very patient and knowledgeable during this process to avoid killing those lovely creatures.

The gravel and any other tank additives must be added initially in order to prepare the fish tank.

To ensure that the water is clear of any harmful bacteria, make sure to thoroughly clean all of these decorations. The tank's preparation process might take anywhere from 24 hours to 4 weeks.

Make sure you wash these substrates without using any soap. The tank should then be filled with dechlorinated water. Fix the lighting and filters. Allow the tank to cycle once more, or until the water starts to fog. then give the cloud time to calm down.

Use that test kit to ensure the water is the right temperature and has a stable pH.

Additionally, make sure the water in the tank is completely clear before adding any additional fish.

In fact, when the aquarium is working properly, some microorganisms aid in the conversion of ammonia to nitrates. Since these bacteria are produced by the fish that are already there, they cannot exist in a fish tank with inactive fish.

The main point of this justification is that there wouldn't be any beneficial bacteria in the tank water if there were no fish around.

The nitrogen cycle is what is known as this. You should be aware that adding fish to the tank will start the nitrogen cycle. Therefore, operating the empty tank for a number of days would be useless.

The fish tank's nitrogen cycle converts harmful compounds that are produced there into beneficial ones by removing the toxic ones. This cycle produces foam, which temporarily clouds the water.

You shouldn't be concerned if this happens because it is a natural process and instead shows that the tank is safe for the fish.

Here are a few straightforward explanations of nitrogen:

1. Like all other living things, fish consume food and produce waste, or excreta.

2. In your aquarium, this waste combines with extra food that collects at the bottom of the tank and plant detritus to produce ammonia.

3. Since ammonia is highly poisonous and hence dangerous for fish, we must propose a technique to break it down.

4. The nitrification of bacteria is this mechanism.

5. These bacteria convert the ammonia in the aquarium into nitrites, which the fish find to be rather bearable.

6. The diverse nitrifying bacteria would then change the nitrites into nitrates, which are even less hazardous for the fish and other aquarium life.

7. Filters are used to capture and reduce these nitrates. In your tank, they would ultimately assemble.

Learn your fish

Here are some fish species that you should put in your aquarium, per my advice:

1. Fish noted for their hardiness, such as barbs, danios, gouramis, and other live bearers, are known for being able to endure the high nitrite and ammonia levels that are produced in a new aquarium.

2. A single fish should be introduced at a time, and the number of fish in the tank should be increased gradually, according to the optimal method. You might also think about starting with one of each of 4 distinct hardy fish species.

3. The fish should be floated in the aquarium for around 15 minutes before being left in the tank, according to the correct manner to add fish to a tank. This would aid in acclimating your fish to the water temperature in its new tank.

4. Make sure you don't add fish bag water to the aquarium because it could be contaminated or occasionally change the temperature and P.H. level of the water there.

5. Give the fish at least two hours to adjust to its new home before feeding it its first meal.

6. Make sure to get food for your first fish as well when you buy it. Keep in mind that the first few times you should only feed modest amounts of the meal.

7. The food that is still there sinks to the bottom and eventually rots away. This spoiled food turns into garbage and produces ammonia, a highly harmful toxin that can kill your fish. So, make an effort to keep as little food as possible. In newly constructed aquariums, especially those without nitrifying bacteria, this must be avoided.

8. The key to doing it successfully is to feed your fish while keeping an eye on them. Put in as little food as it eats in the first 2-3 minutes, and only do this twice per day. Make sure to study the fish label you usually receive when purchasing fish when it comes to eating.

9. Make sure to check the water's pH level every day for the first month.

10. It's time to add some clarifiers to the water if the tank is starting to become hazy.

11. Keep an eye out for any symptoms of stress or illness in your fish.

12. According to a study of the fish's typical behaviour, the energetic fish would swim frequently, while the lethargic ones would typically hover around the water's surface.

13. Therefore, it is necessary to change the water in the tank frequently, especially when it is new. You should think about replacing about 10% of the water in the new fish tank every few days. For at least the first two weeks or so, this must be done.

Fish tank filter

A number of necessary tools, including the heater, the test kit, and the filter, are needed to set up an aquarium.

Fish are typical living creatures that consume food and expel waste. Additionally, certain bacteria grow in water as a natural process. To maintain the water clean and healthy for your cherished pets, the filter in the fish tank removes all these pathogens and undesirable components.

External and internal filtration systems are the two primary categories of filters.

You can easily find aquarium filters at your neighbourhood fish store. Probably not the best location to seek for the filters is your neighbourhood pet store.

Internal Filtration Mechanism

These are employed in both freshwater and saltwater aquariums.

Typically, this tank operates as follows:

1. The salt water aquariums include a tube inside that lets water drain into a sump tank.

2. Your primary tank is immediately below the sump tank.

3. The fish tank's entire water supply is designed to travel through a specific type of foam.

4. Here, all of the garbage and harmful microorganisms gather and filter the water.

5. Finally, a pump raises the water level in the main tank to the top.

6. In every tank, this process is ongoing.

7. This filtration system is highly expensive and noisy, but it is well worth it because it is incredibly effective—in fact, it's regarded as the second best on the market.

8. These filters are generally pricey because they are created specifically for your tank, but frequently they are not worth the high cost.

A big, black internal filter is the third-best product on the market. The way that this functions is as follows:

1. The tank has a massive, rectangular, black structure inside of it.

2. Through its bottom, this rectangular filter absorbs both the waste and water in the tank.

3. The filter then processes this water.

4. It is a filter that is reasonably priced.

System for External Filtration

Since it is the most efficient system on the market, it is also the most expensive. But the cost incurred for these is all that matters.

In essence, this filter is a piece of robust equipment that is installed outside of your fish tank. Although it functions similarly to the two internal filtering systems described above, here the long black tube serves as the connecting component between the tank and the filter.

It is worth every penny spent because it is relatively quiet and very effective.

12 Simple Tips for Caring for Tropical Fish in a Freshwater Aquarium

Only if you give the tropical fish enough care will they be able to live happily in a freshwater aquarium. There might be some significant problems here that are there even though they are not immediately obvious.

So, in order to prolong the life and improve the health of your fish, you should educate yourself in this area.

Your tropical fish might simply survive longer in your fresh water aquarium if you have the appropriate information on fish upkeep.

The following are some essential reminders:

1. Keep in mind that tropical fish can suffer significantly from poor water quality.

2. The tropical fish in your aquarium may suffer severe harm if your aquarium has a lot of algae.

3. Concerns about oxygen deprivation arise when caring for tropical fish in a fresh water aquarium.

4. You must ensure that the water in your freshwater aquarium is balanced if you want to keep your tropical fish healthy.

5. Regularly check the water in the fish tank to make sure it has the right amount of salinity and oxygen.

6. The water testing kits are offered by all neighbourhood pet shops. These are helpful in ensuring that water has the right qualities. At least once each week, these tests must be performed.

7. You must look into the corrective actions if you encounter any issues with the properties' compatibility.

8. Give your fish the right food. Fish food can be found in a wide range on the market.

9. Read the components and the contents before choosing the best fish food for your pets. It is necessary for the fish meal to provide proteins, amino acids, and other vital elements. By doing this, you may be confident that your fishes are eating well, that their digestion is working well, and that their overall colour is being preserved.

10. To determine the proper amount to feed the fish, be sure to read the instruction manual that comes with the fish food.

11. If given too much or too little food, tropical fish could have serious illnesses, just like humans.

12. Verify the aquarium's illumination to ensure that it is suitable for your fish to live a healthy life. The growth of algae in the aquarium picks up speed and may be damaging to your fish if the aquarium is overexposed to direct sunlight or has a lot of light.

12 Creative Tips for Building the Ideal Reef Aquarium

Nature has provided us with a variety of lovely seasonal variations to enjoy, ranging from snow-capped mountains to luscious green landscapes.

There is a whole other world to explore when it comes to the ocean. The beauty of aquatic animals can be magnificent and unimaginable.

The water plants are all distinctively appealing in a similar way.

Numerous investigations and analyses have demonstrated that no two coral reefs are comparable. All of these reefs are unique and incredibly alluring, making everyone who sees them want to take them home with them.

There is no set formula for growing them at home, but it is possible to do so with some work and inventiveness.

You must select from a variety of expensive and affordable ornaments when building that beautiful salt water aquarium.

Finding the ideal balance between creativity, economy, beauty, ecological balance, and financial considerations is ultimately the goal of the game.

To build one of these reefs in your aquarium at home, you must be aware of the following:

1. For your fish to enjoy a healthy life, the aquarium's size needs to be carefully considered and appropriate.

2. Fish require a lot of space to play and swim. Additionally, if different fish breeds are housed in the same tank, they will need additional room to coexist peacefully.

3. Only compatible breeds of fish should be kept together in one tank while choosing your fish, or else a catastrophe could result.

4. The bare minimum you should think about is a 175 gallon tank if you want to set up an optimal eco-system in the fish tank with all natural resources preserved.

5. You are fortunate that pre-drilled aquariums are now available on the market, making it easier than ever to create a picture-perfect reef in your home aquarium. Simply pay a small amount of extra cash to the retailer from which you are buying the aquarium in advance. As opposed to the more conventional hang on the back of the overflowing tanks, this allows you get a really clean look.

6. When deciding how to decorate your aquarium with a natural reef, you have a wide range of options. The experts advise sticking as much as you can to natural ornaments. This would guarantee the wellbeing of your fish, the health of your plants, and the maintenance of the aquarium's ecological balance.

7. A terrific addition to your saltwater aquarium is live rock. This enhances the aquarium's aesthetic appeal and aids in developing the ecosystem of the tank because it is an essential component of the aquatic life. Several micro and macro creatures cover a live rock. These organisms clean the water by filtering out all the waste materials, making it safe for aquatic life.

8. Another lovely addition to saltwater aquariums is live plants. These are practical and offer a variety of facilities for use in the water. The water in the tank is oxygenated by living plants. These give your fish a place to hide, which makes them more playful. In addition to making the fish tank more attractive, they also help to purify the water by absorbing pollutants and adding oxygen. Water and ammonia are broken down by the water plants. The bacteria-containing fraction of the bad or contaminated water is then removed by these plants together with the ammonia. As fish emit a lot of ammonia, plants keep the chemical equilibrium in the fish tank in check.

9. For the ideal reef aquarium, corals are fantastic beautifiers.

10. The experts always suggest that you choose and decide on the breed and type of fish that you would buy before making any purchases or decisions related to your fish tank. This would aid you in choosing items for the aquarium that are acceptable and sensible. For instance, you may pick which fish prefer certain plants based on the breed you have chosen to acquire.

11. To allow the roots of the plants to grow well, the aquarium's bottom layer, which is made up of silt, sand, and/or gravel, needs to be deep enough. While the sort of plant you are putting in there will greatly influence this depth, most plants typically need a depth of about 8 cm.

12.Your salt water aquarium must be lit, like other aquariums, at least during the first half of the day, as both your plants and fish depend on a balanced exchange of oxygen and carbon dioxide. Only with the proper lighting in the aquarium can the plants produce the carbon dioxide they need to survive through photosynthesis. You might also think about placing a device in the fish tank that generates artificial carbon dioxide.

Six Simple Steps for Cleaning a Fresh Water Aquarium

There are many pastimes that one might engage in that may one day become true passions. Keeping an aquarium is one of them. However, this pastime is serious because there is no room for error or you risk hurting or killing a living thing.

Knowing how to properly clean your fresh water aquarium is the first and most important thing you need to know before starting to take care of an aquarium and its fish.

You must be very patient and knowledgeable during this process to avoid killing those lovely creatures.

These pointers would be very helpful to anyone just starting out in this industry.

There are two key things to take into account when cleaning a fresh water aquarium:

- When should the tank be cleaned?

  Why should your tank be cleaned?

The following are the answers to these queries:

Regularly occurring bacteria and other dangerous compounds in the tank's water produce algae, which is extremely damaging to your fish.

Additionally, it might cause illness or even death in your fish. To remove these hazardous algae, you must clean the freshwater fish tank once every two months.

You can offer your fish a clean, safe, and healthy existence by following a few simple procedures. These are listed below:

Step 1: Get the Fish Tank Ready for Cleaning

Emptying the aquarium is certainly the first step in cleaning it. However, emptying the fish tank naturally entails putting your fish somewhere secure outside.

However, leaving your fish in a new location for an extended period of time won't be ideal, so before emptying the fish tank, make sure you have all the supplies you'll need on hand to clean it as quickly as possible.

Therefore, the first thing you set up is an alternative fish tank. It doesn't have to be very big, but it should be big enough to fit all of your fish and give them room to swim. Furthermore, the size of this alternative tank solely depends on the quantity of fish you own.

Here is the list of supplies you will need to clean the tank:

1. To remove your fish from the aquarium, use a fish net.

2. To clean up the spillage, use a towel or paper towels.

3. A bucket or water pitcher to refill the tank

4. Food strainer

5. A spotless sponge

6. A fresh cloth

Removing the Fish from the Tank in Step 2

When taking the fish out of the tank, you must be careful to remember the following:

1. Make sure the substitute container is prepared to receive the fish as well.

2. In order to prevent the fish from going into shock, the water temperature in the substitute container must be nearly identical to that in the fish tank.

3. Put the fish in the new container one by one. This can be accomplished by using a net to capture each fish.

4. Once the alternative container is filled with all the fish, put it somewhere clean and secure where you can be sure the water won't leak.

5. Keep in mind that the fish will move around a lot when you first put them in their new location, which could cause the water to spill. Thus, the container needs to be chosen appropriately. The proper water temperature also significantly lessens these movements.

Step 3: Draining the Fish Tank of Old Water

It's time to dump the fish tank's water after you've removed your fish from it.

Here are some suggestions to make it simple because this task may be the messiest of the entire process:

1. For the purpose of draining the fish tank's water, use a pitcher or small bucket.

2. Put this water in the sink or the toilet.

3. Don't empty the fish tank's water completely.

4. In a fresh water aquarium, you should typically drain around 3/4 of the water.

5. The remaining one-fourth aids in the acclimatisation of the additional water that you will add later.

Step 4: Emptying and cleaning the Tank's Gravel

The gravel at the bottom of the fish tank is where the majority of the filth and waste accumulate. So cleaning it thoroughly is crucial. Here are some quick guidelines for cleaning gravel:

1. First, empty the tank of all the gravel.

2. You can utilise the following tools for this:

- a small net,

- a dust pan, and

- a little scoop

3. Now put the gravel in a sieve of some sort.

4. Put this gravel-filled strainer in the hot water.

5. Rinse the gravel continuously to remove any particles or garbage that may have settled on top of it.

6. Now set it carefully aside because we'll be adding to the fish tank later.

Cleaning Your Tank is Step Five.

1. This procedure include cleaning the tank's interior. Here are some pointers for doing that:

2. The major task here is to clear out the algae that has accumulated inside the tank.

3. When the water in the tank is too warm or the fish tank is exposed to direct sunlight, algae grows.

4. You should use a scratch pad to remove the algac, but be careful to select one that is not too abrasive or you risk scratching the fish tank's glass.

5. When cleaning the glass, use hot water to more effectively eliminate the algae.

6. Always keep in mind that cleaning the fish tank's glass with any kind of cleanser or detergent is extremely damaging to the fish.

7. You must use a towel or soft rag to wipe the remainder of your tank after the algae have been removed. Keep in mind that you might need to say this out loud several times.

8. While cleaning, be careful to constantly rinse the rag or towel to get rid of all the trash.

9. If you have any decorative items in your tank, thoroughly wash and rinse them with hot water.

10. Verify once more that there are no wastes or accumulations inside the tank.

Step 6: Repositioning the Tank

Once everything inside the tank has been thoroughly cleaned and dried, it's time to put everything back in its original locations. Here are some procedures for carrying out the same:

1. Place the gravel first, working your way from back to front.

2. The tank should then be filled with water.

3. Verify the water's temperature to ensure that it is the same as your normal one.

4. Try adding water that is the same temperature as the one you need to get at the very end.

5. Reinstall all of the decorative elements in the fish tank.

6. Place your fish back in their tank at this time.

7. Even though it could take some time for your fish to adjust to the new environment, you have now taken all necessary precautions to make sure the water is safe for your fish.

You should also keep in mind the following advice:

1. Every two months, the fish tank needs to be cleaned.

2. Always maintain the tank's filters clean. Never leave them dirty; always clean them or replace them.

3. Cleaning would be easier if you changed 20% or less of the fish tank's water each month, which is what is required to be done.

4. It is essential to keep your aquarium clean and secure at all times if you want to have a healthy fish tank and content fish.

5. This would not only give your pets more beauty and life, but it would also make your aquarium a lovely sight to behold for everyone.

20 Simple Tips for Caring for the Freshwater Guppy in an Aquarium

The guppy is perhaps the fish that people love to keep the most in fresh water aquariums. These have their own requirements to live healthily even though they are not particularly difficult to maintain.

The following advice can help your guppies enjoy longer, happier lives filled with health and happiness:

1. These fish thrive in hard water and can easily adjust to slight changes in the water's quality. Nevertheless, you must reduce the oscillations because they stress your fish.

2. The ideal water temperature for an aquarium housing guppy fish is between 72 and 82 degrees.

3. The ideal pH range for aquarium homing guppies is between 7.0 and 8.2.

4. In comparison to other tropical and marine fish, the requirements for keeping guppies are fairly simple.

5. Guppies develop quickly. They often measure 1.5 to 2 inches long when fully mature.

6. The aquarium is made rather intriguing and lovely by these tiny fish with tails that resemble feathery fans.

7. Being fairly playful, guppies are a lot of pleasure to watch as they swim around the aquarium.

8. Food is an absolute necessity for all living things. Guppies can eat almost everything, so you need to be aware of that. However, frozen and flakes meals are their preferred cuisine.

9. A guppy needs to be fed roughly three times per day.

10. Make sure to give it very little food at a time.

11. Provide it with its favourite food, especially when the babies are present because guppies have a tendency to consume their young when there is a lack of food.

12. The guppy fish require routine water changes just like any other aquarium inhabitants. Though it must be done once every week or twice a month, the clear sign that it's time to replace the water is when it begins to smell or becomes hazy.

13. Change only one-third of the water at a time. Fish would experience less stress as a result of the water changes being reduced for them.

14. Your pet will instantly become healthy if you make it happy. Your guppies would be quite content if you created a setting that felt really homey. Add different kinds of plants where they can hide, for example.

15. Think about keeping your tank's substrate between 1 and 2 inches thick.

16. The colourful pebbles and the dead, crushed coral are adored by guppies. These two would make the aquarium aesthetically pleasing and make your guppies happy.

17. There are several well-known guppies to pick from, including Flagtail, Fantail, Deltatail, Spadetail, and Roundtail. Guppies are renowned for their lovely, extraordinary, and distinctive tails, which make up close to one-third of their entire bodies.

18. Guppies are the easiest prey due to their fragile and long tail, thus keep this in mind when keeping them in an aquarium alongside other breeds of fish. So be cautious about the breeds you mix it with.

19. Guppies may breed with other fish, and they do so frequently—every three to four weeks. As a result, an aquarium might be crowded quickly.

20. If you don't want to cross-breed your fish, just keep them in separate aquariums.

A Guide to Aquarium Fish Care: Over 20 Simple Tips for New Owners

When you are certain that you want to get a fish aquarium, you must be aware of the proper tools and extras that will improve the lifetime and wellbeing of your fish and tank.

These add-ons consist of:

1. Heaters

2. Buffers

3. Filters

4. Gravel

5. Floss

6. meals, etc.

You must also be aware of all the procedures and recommendations for maintaining a clean aquarium and healthy fish in order to guarantee the hygiene of your fish.

Always do your study before buying fish and an aquarium, experts advise.

You can take good care of your fish and the aquarium by following these helpful tips:

1. **Ornaments**: Decorations that enhance aesthetics and provide a lively environment for your fish.

2. **You can pick between real and artificial plants**. Even while live plants require a lot of maintenance, they serve a variety of purposes for your fish.

3. **Gravel** - The aquarium's foundation is made of gravel. The amount of fish you add to the aquarium, the plants you add, and other variables all affect how deep this layer is.

4. **Test kits** - These are useful for periodically checking the aquarium's water.

5. **Water treatment systems** are very important to keep the water clean because otherwise, the ammonia and bacteria that are always accumulating in the water may kill your fish without warning.

6. **Food** - Fishes need food, just like all other living things do, therefore you must have a plentiful supply on hand for your aquarium inhabitants. Make sure to read the ingredients on the fish food you buy and give it to the fish as directed in the information you receive about the fish.

7. **Heater Accessories** - You would need to install a heater in the fish tank in order to maintain the water's temperature. If you're thinking about keeping some tropical fish, you absolutely must purchase this.

You must ensure that the heater's size fits the fish tank before making the purchase. It must not occupy much room, or your fish will become uncomfortable in the tank. Additionally, keep in mind that there are numerous heater types available; you must know which one best meets your needs.

Here is the aquarium construction process:

1. Fill a bucket with water first, then rinse the pebbles to remove any dirt, filth, or bacteria.

2. When the gravel has been cleaned, add water to your tank.

3. Add the remaining half of the water that the tank actually needs.

4. The aquarium's decorations and plants should then be added.

5. This completes the aquarium's need for additions.

6. Finally, fill the tank to the desired level with water.

7. Use the instruction manual that came with your tank now. Fill your tank correctly by adhering to the guidelines provided in this manual.

8. Place the heating and filter systems in the tank next.

9. Follow the directions in the handbook you were given when you received the heater and filters in order to install them safely and effectively.

10. The water treatment system is then added to the tank. By doing this, dangerous substances in the water, such as copper, metal, and other associated elements, are removed.

11. Now either utilise specific materials that allow you to do that safely before adding the fish to the tank, or else we advise you to wait at least a few weeks before adding life to your tank.

12. There are some naturally occurring microorganisms in a tank of water. To keep your fish healthy and secure, the water needs to be filtered to remove these microorganisms. Once the aquarium's water has settled, use your test kit to see if it is completely clean or not. You should also check that the water is the proper temperature and that all of its chemicals are in balance.

13. Add your fish in small amounts after the water in the tank has been checked one last time.

14. Always choose the peaceful fish for your aquarium over the aggressive ones. The most suitable passive fish for beginners are goldfish, otocinclus, plecostemas, etc. These keep the aquarium clean and are very simple to maintain.

Salt Water Aquarium: 11 Tips for Creating a Beautiful Display

The aquatic world offers some truly fascinating and exciting views. For the observers, it is certainly a whole different world. The desire to bring this beauty home is common among many aquatic aficionados.

You do not, however, need to build a 20-foot tropical aquarium in your home or convert your living room into a room for a live shark in order to bring this beauty home.

The scenic magnificence of the Baltimore National Aquarium can be imagined right in your own home! Your salt water aquarium at home might use some artistic aquascaping to achieve the same results as Baltimore's experts!

The key is to choose the appropriate decorations and arrange them properly in your tank.

Here are a few simple pointers for the same:

1. You have the option of choosing between real and plastic plant accessories to adorn your aquarium. In any case, bringing Mother Nature inside is made easier by employing the real plants and other creatures in the aquarium.

2. You must also be aware that the decorations you add to the aquarium will be used by your fish. They would seek solace and amusement in them. Therefore, it is always recommended to use real aquatic plants for the benefit of your pets and to preserve the beautiful sense of your aquarium.

3. Spending time and effort finding the ideal aquarium's décor and ornaments is worth it because a well-decorated salt water aquarium is a valuable treasure for many years. The neighbourhood tropical fish dealer can be really helpful because he can supply you with a variety of decorations for your saltwater fish tank.

4. A terrific addition to your saltwater aquarium is live rock. This enhances the aquarium's aesthetic appeal and aids in developing the ecosystem of the tank because it is an essential component of the aquatic life. Several micro and macro creatures cover a live rock. These organisms clean the water by filtering out all the waste materials, making it safe for aquatic life.

5. Sand and driftwood enhance the salt water aquarium's grandeur, beauty, and appeal. Additionally, these are necessary components for the natural habitat of saltwater fish.

6. Another lovely addition to saltwater aquariums is live plants. These are practical and offer a variety of facilities for use in the water. The water in the tank is oxygenated by living plants. These give your fish a place to hide, which makes them more playful.

7. If you're lucky, your fish may lay their eggs in these plants.

8. The experts always suggest that you choose and decide on the breed and type of fish that you would buy before making any purchases or decisions related to your fish tank. This would aid you in choosing items for the aquarium that are acceptable and sensible. For instance, you may pick which fish prefer certain plants based on the breed you have chosen to acquire.

9. Salt water plants require specialised care and attention, which can be provided with advance planning.

10. Your salt water aquarium must be lit, like other aquariums, at least during the first half of the day, as both your plants and fish depend on a balanced exchange of oxygen and carbon dioxide. Only with the proper lighting in the aquarium can the plants produce the carbon dioxide they need to survive through photosynthesis. You might also think about placing a device in the fish tank that generates artificial carbon dioxide.

11. To allow the roots of the plants to grow well, the aquarium's bottom layer, which is made up of silt, sand, and/or gravel, needs to be deep enough. While the sort of plant you are putting in there will greatly influence this depth, most plants typically need a depth of about 8 cm.

Aquarium and Fish Care: 30 Things to Keep in Mind

There are many pastimes that one might engage in that may one day become true passions. Keeping an aquarium is one of them. However, this pastime is serious because there is no room for error or you risk hurting or killing a living thing.

The nearby library, the World Wide Web, or the internet are the best places to learn everything there is to know about your fish and the aquarium that serves as their home.

Online, a variety of beginning kits are accessible. Additionally, you'll find a tonne of information on some starter fish to get you started with this fascinating hobby.

Here are some important reminders before delving into this fascinating area:

1. You must comprehend the nitrogen cycle in order to properly maintain your fish tank. Ammonia, nitrites, and nitrates are all involved in this cycle.

These substances are naturally produced by fish in the water they inhabit. It's your responsibility to maintain the proper balance of these chemicals to keep the water safe for your fish to survive.

2. Ammonia balance in the water is a challenge for newcomers to this activity. In that scenario, you might think about relying on the internet starter kits. Ammonia is one of the ingredients in these kits. In essence, these kits give you a way to intentionally regulate the amount of ammonia in the fish tank.

3. These kits also provide instructions and, on occasion, suitable starting fishes. These fish make a sufficient amount of ammonia on their own.

4. The greatest choice would be to have a goldfish if you are starting with a coldwater tank.

5. Make sure there are enough plants in your fish tank. In addition to making the fish tank more attractive, they also help to purify the water by absorbing pollutants and adding oxygen.

6. Water and ammonia are broken down by the water plants. The bacteria-containing fraction of the bad or contaminated water is then removed by these plants together with the ammonia.

7. As fish emit a lot of ammonia, plants keep the chemical equilibrium in the fish tank in check.

8. Be absolutely certain about the amount of food you are giving the fish when you are ammonizing your aquarium with the starting fish. Keep in mind that the first few times you should only feed modest amounts of the meal.

9. The food that is still there sinks to the bottom and eventually rots away. This food goes bad and produces compounds that are so toxic they can kill your fish. Therefore, make an effort to keep the fewest amount of food. The key to doing it successfully is to feed your fish while keeping an eye on them. Put in as little food as it eats in the first 2-3 minutes, and only do this twice per day. Make sure to study the fish label you usually receive when purchasing fish when it comes to eating.

10. Use the test kits correctly, and make sure to check the water's ammonia level once a week at regular intervals.

11. A proper ammonization procedure often takes 5 weeks or more.

12. Make sure you buy the appropriate stand to set up the fish tank before you buy it.

13. Keep in mind that the fish tank should not be placed near heaters or direct sunlight as this will encourage the growth of algae, which will kill your fish.

14.When adding gravel to the fish tank, make sure it is completely clean. If you bought cooked gravel, give it a thorough rinse before putting it to the tank. If not, you must first boil it before rinsing it and adding it to the tank.

15.The correct approach to add gravel to a fish tank is to start at the back and work your way forward.

16. The type of fish and filter you use will determine the height of the gravel you put. This is more pertinent to the tank's front. The gravel layer in the tank's front needs to be very thin.

17. If you were to use under-gravel filters, the gravel layer up front would be extremely thin.

18. The final step in setting up the fish tank should be to install the filters and heaters. However, if a motorised filter is something you're thinking about employing, you must install the filter before adding the gravel.

19. The next stage is to add plants and other decorations after the gravel has been placed. To maintain the purity of the water in the tank, be careful to rinse these additives well.

20. Choose exclusively marine-based plants, if possible.

21. Only half of the necessary amount should initially be poured into the tank. Utilize pre-treated water as you halfway fill the tank.

22. Once all of the components have been added, you can completely fill it with water.

23. Keep a constant check on the water's temperature with a thermometer after adding all the necessary water to the tank.

24. Place the filters in the fish tank at this point.

25. You can put goldfish in your aquarium before you start the ammonization procedure. If you want to buy any other fish, you must wait a few weeks for the ammonization process in the fish tank to be finished.

26. Additionally, make sure the water in the tank is completely clear before adding any additional fish.

27. A single fish should be introduced at a time, and the number of fish in the tank should be increased gradually, according to the optimal method. You might also think about starting with one of each of 4 distinct hardy fish species.

28. The fish should be floated in the aquarium for around 15 minutes before being left in the tank, according to the correct manner to add fish to a tank. This would aid in acclimating your fish to the water temperature in its new tank.

29. Make sure you don't add fish bag water to the aquarium because it could be contaminated or occasionally change the temperature and P.H. level of the water there.

30. Verify that the aquarium has the appropriate level of lighting. Along with these lights, there is a cowl that can be placed over the aquarium's top. The majority of aquariums today include a hood, which is a reality. Actually, the hood protects the fish inside the tank and keeps animals out. The lights within the tank are likewise controlled by the hood.

Aquarium Fish Care for Carp

People have long liked keeping carp as pets. The pH, temperature, and diet of the water are just a few elements that contribute to a healthy living habitat for carp. Carp have long been associated with Asia as a symbol of virility, beauty, and strength. Today, we'll look at a few local species and offer advice on how to take care of carps.

The Asiatic Tooth carp is a fish of extraordinary wonder that lives in a variety of settings, including streams, ponds, and drainage regions.

Asiatic tooth carp prefer water that is typically between 70 and 80 degrees Fahrenheit, going by the scientific names Genera Aplochelilus and Oryzias. Carp live close to the water's surface and dislike highly alkaline or extremely hard water.

Asiatic tooth carp may easily reach mosquito larvae and other relevant food sources since they reside close to the surface. While carp occasionally eat and love dry fish diets, it's crucial to maintain giving them part of their natural food while they're in captivity.

These carp love residing in small to medium-sized tanks with a maximum water capacity of 10 gallons. They really enjoy water that is somewhat acidic, relatively hard, and where organic deposits can grow easily. High peat content waters should contain floating plants, fine gravel without lime, and plants with fine leaves.

Spawning Procedure

The spawn that the tooth carp generates develops quite quickly. The tooth carp will lay a few eggs and mate every day for a period of three weeks.

The adults won't harm the young while they are still in the spawning stage, but once the larvae hatch and become fry, the adults will consume their own young.

Remove the parents from the tank before the larvae hatch if you want to save some of the fry. The larvae can also be taken out and put in a separate aquarium with lots of plants. Usually, people choose the first option because it is simpler.

When the eggs hatch, you should separate the fry by size and get rid of a couple to stop cannibalism.

The Green Panchex Dwarf

Some people also refer to the near relative of the tooth carp, the dwarf of Green Panchax, as Panchax Parvus. The fish belongs to the Aplocheilus Blocki group and is typically found in the seas near Ceylon and India.

The mature Green Dwarf measures 1 3/4" long, making it the ideal aquarium fish. The fish is a greenish-yellow tint with red and yellow stripes along its body. Since the fish's native home waters are warm, tank water is ideal for it.

Typically, they will consume both live and dried meals. Make sure the water is 78 degrees before breeding dwarfs.

Using two males and a tiny harem of females is the key to effectively breeding dwarfs.

Medaka the Geisha

The cousin of the Dwarf of Green Panchax, the Geisha Girl Medaka, whose scientific name is Oryzias latipes, arrives from further east, in Japan. Due to its nationality, it is also known as the Ricefish or Japanese Medaka.

Its resemblance to Japan's staple food, rice, which is nearly colourless, may also help to explain why it is known as the "Ricefish." The fish measures around half an inch long.

The females are easier to identify since they are smaller and rounder than the males and have rounded fins. For the Medaka, slightly acidic waters work best.

To balance the pH if your water is acidic, it is advised that you add around 1 teaspoon of salt to 3 litres of water.

The Geisha Girl Medaka can survive in water that is 75 degrees or 80 degrees in temperature. However, 78 degrees is the ideal temperature.

The Geish Girl medaka does not consume pickles as far as diet is concerned. She will consume practically anything.

Aquarium for Catfish and Fish Care

There are numerous species and origins for catfish throughout the world. Here are some fundamental details regarding catfishes, including information on how to care for them in a tank.

There are numerous varieties of the catfish, which scientists refer to as the Siluridae. The name "Glass Catfish" comes from Asia, specifically from India, and refers to both the fish's nearly transparent body and the translucent coating that covers it.

Although there are other catfish species, they are not as attractive as the Glass catfish for aquarium use.

The fish is about 3 1/2" inches long and is known as a catfish because of the noticeable "whiskers" on its top lip. Barbells are another name for these whiskers.

The Mirror Catfish are not really gregarious creatures; they prefer to blend in and don't move around much. Catfish typically eat near the water's surface and prefer to consume living things.

They are known for being scavengers and have a reputation for not being particularly fussy eaters, making them a very useful fish. Being a resilient fish, they are not greatly impacted by changes in water temperature, alkalinity, or acidity.

Catfish consume a variety of other rotting materials in addition to other dead fish. They eat a variety of photo-synthetic organisms, such as algae. Having a fish like this in your aquarium will aid in preventing the growth of algae.

The skeletal system of catfish is different from that of many other fish in that it is formed of bone as opposed to cartilage. The catfish has bones in place of the soft fins that many other fish have.

Again, the catfish lacks scales in contrast to many of its aquatic neighbours. Its whiskers enable it to smell and taste in addition to responding to touch.

From the Belgian Congo comes the upside-down catfish. As an adult, the fish can grow to reach 2 inches long. This fish stands out because it seems to be swimming backwards.

This is due to the fact that the whiskers are related to the chin and point upward, although the eye is really below the mouth. It swims right side up even though it appears to be swimming upside down.

Because it is a scavenger and will help keep the amount of algae in your tank to a minimal, this catfish is perfect for living in a tank with other fish.

The Electric Catfish is another another animal that is quite intriguing. While it can grow to reach 10 feet long in open seas, an aquarium will only support growth of two feet. This fish can be found in the west and centre of Africa among lakes, rivers, and streams.

Although this fish has a cylindrical body and no dorsal fin, it makes up for this lack with a large, robust adipose fin. It is not a good idea to mix it with other fish in your aquarium since it will shock anyone who gets too close.

Although not quite as strong or violent, the shock is comparable to that of an electric eel. However, the shock is more powerful than the Mormyridae's.

The main components of the electric catfish's diet include flesh, worms, and fish that are smaller than it. It is renowned for being a nocturnal animal that consumes a lot of food.

Water pH and temperature are not major issues with many catfish species. This man is content as long as he has access to plenty of food and drink.

Coral Reef Care Aquarium Tanks

You can be tempted to invest more money in the most exquisite, expensive fish species and the most expensive crustaceans or shrimp when you want to build the aquarium of your dreams.

It looks intriguing to create an entire underwater world that is alive with amazing colour and beauty. However, if you want to start an aquarium hobby, this is definitely not the greatest place to start.

Coral reef aquariums need far more upkeep and maintenance than merely freshwater or saltwater aquariums need. Freshwater fish are a better location to start since they can typically survive changes in pH and water temperature better than other marine species.

You generally shouldn't try to start a coral reef aquarium unless you are very passionate about the pastime and have a lot of experience.

Before the ideal water pH is attained and the ideal lighting and water temperature are established, it can take several months. Start by mixing regular tap water with sea salt, which is available at many pet stores.

The tank's salinity should be between 1.023 and 1.004 at all times. Keep the temperature in a coral reef aquarium between 75 and 79 degrees for best results. The most crucial element of the entire procedure is the pH. This tank's pH should be between 8.3 and 8.4, which is the optimal range.

You can get pH testing kits online or at your neighbourhood pet store. Chemicals that can be used to modify the pH levels in the tank are also available at the pet store.

The ph level has very little margin for error, so it's crucial that you take your time and make sure all the pieces are in place. Otherwise, a mistake could cost you a lot of money.

Under no circumstances add marine life to the tank before making sure everything is in order.

Introduce the anemones and clown fish after everything is flawless. That's correct, begin with Nemo. The toughest organisms that live on reefs are he and anemones.

Keep a watchful check on the wildlife and watch for any indications of stress. Fish illnesses are primarily a result of stress. These critters were removed directly from their natural home and put in your tank, so it could take some time for them to get used to the surroundings.

Crowding is another significant stress-related factor. Allow 10 gallons of water per inch of fish, being cautious to consider the fish's final size rather than its size at the time of purchase.

About 30 days pass before the fish begin to exhibit symptoms of illness. If everything is well and the fish seem to have settled in after about a month, you can start introducing more marine species.

Be careful to chose new species for the tank carefully based on how well-suited they will be to the other animals inside.

Because they get along well, species like the dwarf angelfish or mandarin fish might be a good addition to the clown fish tank.

Along with being compatible with the water's pH and temperature, the fish must also be compatible with their food source, which is even more crucial.

Make sure the present tank inhabitants have enough time to become used to their new surroundings and tank mates. The best strategy to create a fantastic marine aquarium is to conduct extensive research to determine which animals are suitable with your current collection.

You can be proud of your fantastic aquarium once you put in the necessary time and work.

Aquarium Establishment: Live Rocks

Aquariums have the ability to take people to a world of wonder and beauty, even if they may never get the chance to see the wonderful majesty of life beneath the sea.

Therefore, a well-kept aquarium that is stocked with as many of the species that make up a reef and its natural environs can provide a breathtaking journey into a world of great diversity, colour, shape, and variety.

It is true that an excellent reef aquarium should be treasured and sought after. A nice addition to the undersea habitat you design can be live rocks.

Simply put, a live rock is a rock. The rock is a living rock because of what lives there, though.

The aquarium can benefit greatly from the inclusion of macro- and microorganisms that digest the waste produced by fish and other animals and are therefore essential to the ecology.

But it's not as simple as throwing a rock in the aquarium and praying for the best. To ensure that the advantages for the aquarium and the live rock are as good as they can be, a method needs to be understood and followed.

A live rock can be cured relatively easily, but this crucial step must be completed properly. In the absence of this, the tank's ammonia level can increase, endangering or even killing the fish. Selecting a container big enough to hold the rock you want to cure is the first step in the curing process.

After that, add saltwater to the container. After that, add a heater and a water pump to the "tank" to manage the temperature and circulation. Remove the heater and half of the water as soon as the water reaches the right temperature.

After that, carefully clean the rock by stirring it in saltwater in a separate bucket, taking care to get rid of as many loose creatures and detritus as you can.

Take the rock that has been cleaned and drop it into the ready-made water. Reinstall the heater and pump, then allow nature to do its thing. The entire procedure is complete when there is no longer any odour of ammonia and there is zero ammonia in the water.

It is now secure to place the rock in the tank and allow Nature to carry out her tasks with a fully natural filtering mechanism made possible by a live rock.

Coldwater Aquarium and Freshwater Fish Care

The ideal fish to start a collection with are freshwater species because they are more resilient to changes in pH and water temperature. It needs fresh water with plenty of oxygen because it is still a fish.

And fish produce natural wastes just like every other living creature does. Effective waste management can prevent the wastes from eventually harming the fish. Ammonia causes oxygen levels to drop, which is why you should also add other living organisms to your aquarium that can absorb these wastes in addition to a filter.

Like many other plants above the surface, underwater plants also produce oxygen as they develop, making them a wonderful addition to any freshwater aquarium.

When purchasing your tank, you should think about the type of light, hood, stand, and thermometer you want to use. Both the temperature of the water and the growth of the plants may be affected by these.

How to select the ideal aquarium

Aquarium volumes are expressed in terms of quarts or cubic decimeters. The decent tanks come in sizes that vary from 45 litres on up to a maximum of 130 litres. These tanks are frequently distinguished by their length and depth as well as by how simple they are to clean.

Additionally, you may keep a variety of fresh water fish in the same tank at the same time without any problems. Additionally, there is much of space for growth.

Selecting a strong stand

You must take a number of variables into account in order to make an informed choice regarding the aquarium stand you should purchase. These considerations include whether it can handle the weight of both the tank and the water it holds.

Will the tank be on level ground or will it require some sort of levelling? Should the stand be connected to additional sources of support to make it stronger as well?

Selecting the appropriate type of light

The health of the plants in your tank depends on the lights. The only major issue they create is the accumulation of algae, which you must regularly remove lest the water's cleanliness start to decline.

Additionally, the lights generate a lot of heat, which could modify the water's temperature. Finding a balance between a light that is bright enough for plants to grow and one that won't put the fish in the tank through unnecessary stress due to the heat they produce is crucial when thinking about lights.

The significance of selecting a quality hood

The device known as the hood serves as the tank's lid and prevents fish from jumping out and drowning on the floor. Additionally, it prevents undesirable animals, trash, dirt, and other contaminants from entering the tank.

It also protects your light. For the best protection for your aquarium, be sure to purchase a hood that is the same size as your tank.

Choosing the proper thermometer type

A thermometer measures the temperature of the air or water in the surrounding area. They typically contain mercury or alcohol and are made from glass tubes. The level inside the thermometer changes based on whether the temperature is rising or falling.

These thermometers are likely to be available at your neighbourhood pet store. All you truly need is probably something really basic, which you can purchase.

For your tank, in addition to everything that has been said up to this point, you should have gravel, heaters, filters, and the like. You can also buy the right kind of food from your neighbourhood pet store.

Aquarium Filters and Their Use

The filtration system in your aquarium is crucial because of the waste products released by fish and from other unnatural sources. In addition to keeping your fish healthy, it will also make your aquarium look more attractive. They come in a variety of forms, from natural filters to more chemical or mechanical ones.

Biodegradable filters

Through a process called as denitrification, these filters convert the nitrogen in the water into ammonia, nitrites, and nitrogen. Fish can be harmful to ammonia and nitrites, but because something toxic has been converted into something less toxic, fish are able to adapt to nitrites.

When put to the tank, enriched soil bacteria start turning ammonia into nitrates. The nitrogen produced by the reaction is converted into substances that provide natural resources.

Mechanical filters are another option, and they purge water of solid waste and particles in a variety of ways. Filtration cartridges made of foam, floss, or pebbles are a few examples. For some filters to function effectively, you need both of those.

Chemical filtering systems employ carbon activation. The technology seeks to remove water softeners and ammonia from the water.

It's crucial to clean the water in your tank. Particularly considering that the water is tap or groundwater and that the fish's general health depends on the water's quality. Systematic water filtration can lessen the amount of chemicals in your water.

Corner filtration, motorised outdoor filters, under-gravel filtration, and foam canister flow-through filtration are all types of aquarium filters.

The Operation of the Filter

One of the more popular types of filtering involves the delivery of forced air and is known as corner filtration. A weak vacuum is used to eliminate the air; this forces the water through the filter and the floss inside the filter.

In addition to catching large particles of pollution, floss also successfully cleans the tank by inhibiting bacterial development and removing a significant amount of very minute algae due to its fibrous texture.

Basically, it allows the water to breathe. However, due to the fact that wet floss is so thick, charcoal gravel is also put in the filter to promote flow and the charcoal itself also serves as a filtering agent. The end result is actually superior on all fronts.

Electrically powered pumps, also referred to as externally powered filters, draw enormous volumes of water through the filter and through the floss and charcoal.

The pump can maintain more or a wider variety of fish than many other filters and does provide for ventilation in the tank. Any filter must be regularly cleaned and changed in order to retain its efficacy; otherwise, performance will degrade.

Placing gravel in the bottom of your tank is one approach to enhance filtration. In fact, some of the undesirable particles in the water are strained out by the filtering systems that can be put beneath the gravel.

Although it is a non-chemical filter, there are certain drawbacks. All the fish in a tank can be cared for by pumps, but not by this filtration system. Additionally, extremely regular maintenance must be given to the canisters used to catch particles and the foam filtration components for the air supply.

These canisters include mechanical, chemical, and biological filters, but are sadly ineffective and typically not advised over the long term because appropriate water conditioning is still necessary in addition to all the attention provided to the filter.

Aquarium Bubble Coral Maintenance

Today, an increasing number of people choose to install saltwater aquariums and frequently utilise coral as part of the decor of their surroundings.

It is crucial to understand that coral is a live organism just like any other fish or creature you might add before buying it and adding it to your habitat. Because of this, it's crucial to know how to take care of and adapt this fascinating critter to your tank.

One of the more common and well-liked coral species that people buy for their aquariums is bubble coral. Due of its widespread use, it will serve as both a model and a guidance for coral care in this article.

Bubble coral, pearl bubbler coral, and grapen bubble coral are the three main subspecies.

The future emphasis will simply be on "bubble coral" because all of these issues can be resolved in quite similar ways. The secret is realising that coral will need to develop and expand, just like any other fish or critter you put in your tank.

These tentacle-like appendages on bubble coral only emerge at night to assist the coral in feeding. These coral could potentially sting other coral if they are kept in close proximity to one another while eating.

Make sure to leave at least 6 inches between each piece of coral when deciding where to place it in your aquarium. Be sure to consider the amount of light the coral is exposed to.

Any bubble coral will thrive anywhere in the tank if you add additional lights in addition to the one inside the tank hood.

If you're considering using fluorescent lights, it might be a good idea to position the coral closer to the top of the tank. Furthermore, bubble coral dislikes a lot of water movement.

In fact, if the coral is placed in some sort of current, the vesicles won't open, which could result in the coral's demise.

Considering that the coral, like your fish or other tank inhabitants, is a living organism. They require a lot of the same feeding and care.

The sphere Bits of shrimp and clams once or twice a week are to Coral's liking. Place the food where the coral can reach it with its tentacles by taking it there. The coral will consume whatever food that its tentacles grasp right away.

Overfeeding a coral can cause algae to start to build up on the coral, so use caution. That may cause coral to suffer and even perish.

Therefore, take extra care to regularly clear the algae. Another adversary of coral are flat worms. They are simple to recognise and see. On the coral, they appear as rounded coral patches.

Nevertheless, they are not very dangerous and don't do much harm.

However, you must take action if you spot a lot of them. Otherwise, there can be a fatal outcome. Many individuals don't know how to take care of coral, a beautiful organism that can enhance the attractiveness of your aquatic habitat.

The benefits of learning as much as you can about this fascinating species will far outweigh the time invested. There will be a variety of marine life in your aquarium in addition to fish and other common species. The bubble coral can serve as the foundation for a stunning underwater scene.

Conclusion

As I've demonstrated in this book, taking care of aquariums may be easy if you follow a few simple success strategies. To preserve water quality and get rid of contaminants, regular partial water changes are crucial. Additionally, providing your fish with a range of nutritious diets will keep them healthy and disease-resistant. Third, keeping your aquarium clean on a regular basis will keep your fish healthy and the water quality high. You can take pleasure in a lovely, healthy aquarium for many years by adhering to these easy suggestions.

I wish you much success in your aquarium adventure!

Troy Ludo, Author and Loving Aquarium Owner